THE ANTHOLOGY OF THE RIO GRANDE VALLEY INTERNATIONAL POETRY FESTIVAL

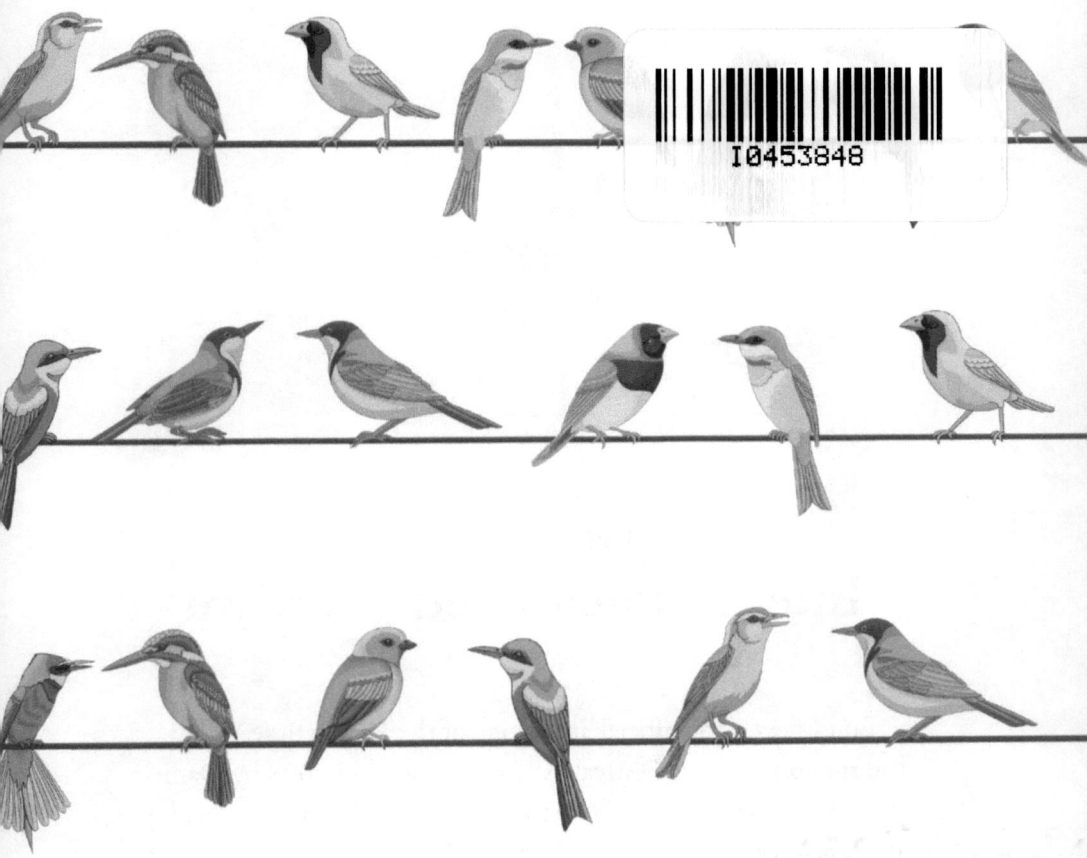

BOUNDLESS
2025

Selected & Edited by
JAVIER VILLARREAL & EDWARD VIDAURRE

V.I.P.F.

Rio Grande Valley International Poetry Festival

Boundless is the official anthology of the Rio Grande Valley International Poetry Festival (VIPF), founded in 2008 by Daniel García Ordaz and Brenda Nettles Riojas. VIPF is held annually the last weekend in April in deep South Texas as a celebration of National Poetry Month.

www.valleypoetryfest.org

THE ANTHOLOGY OF THE RIO GRANDE VALLEY INTERNATIONAL POETRY FESTIVAL

FLOWERSONG
PRESS

BOUNDLESS
2025

Selected & Edited by
JAVIER VILLARREAL & EDWARD VIDAURRE

FLOWERSONG
PRESS

FlowerSong Press
McAllen, Texas 78501
Copyright © 2025 FlowerSong Press

ISBN: 978-1-963245-97-4

Published by FlowerSong Press
in the United States of America.
www.flowersongpress.com

Set in Adobe Garamond Pro

Edited by Javier Villarreal and Edward Vidaurre
Cover Design by Priscilla Celina Suarez
Book Images by Anisa Onofre

NOTICE: SCHOOLS AND BUSINESSES
FlowerSong Press offers copies of this book at quantity discount with bulk
purchase for educational, business, or sales promotional use. For information,
please email the Publisher at info@flowersongpress.com.

Table of Contents

II. Boundless Youth Poetry

About the Art in this Anthology

The art in this anthology is by Anisa Onofre. Anisa is a sketchbook artist and painter in San Antonio, Texas. She works at Gemini Ink as Publications Director and is a co-publisher at Aztlan Libre Press.

Dedication

IN HONOR OF:

Jan Seale. 2012 Texas State Poet Laureate, McAllen, Texas
Emmy Pérez, 2020 Texas Poet Laureate, McAllen, Texas
Daniel García Ordaz, 2023-25 City of McAllen Poet Laureate

IN MEMORIAM:

Dr. Gloria Evangelina Anzaldúa
Jovita González
Dr. Américo Paredes
Raúl R. Salinas
Trinidad Sánchez

So You Don't Love to Read
Xochitl-Julisa Bermejo

I was never a reader. I have no stories of the library being my favorite place. I have no memory of losing myself in a book, though I could have used the escape. As the youngest of four children and the only girl in a working-class Mexican household, books were not part of my world. Between the demands of a working mom, emotionally distant father, and four ravenous children aged teens to grade-schoolers, yelling is what filled our home day and night. Yelling to get food on the table. Yelling to pick up messes. Yelling about money. Yelling about family. Yelling over the Atari console.

"¿Quien rompió la lámpara?" my father would yell. My three brothers and I remained silent to avoid what came after yelling.

"Why ask? None of them are going to say!" my mother would yell back. My eldest two teenage brothers were growing into their bodies and full of rage. Sometimes yelling would explode into shoving. Holes decorated the walls and doors as evidence.

Once a fight started while we were all in the car together returning from a family party. My father was drunk and driving. He accused his two teenage sons of being ungrateful. They railed against the accusation. My mom kept quiet. Back at the house the fighting became physical. My eldest brother ran off. My mom took the rest of us away from my father and into the night. We walked down the street and called an aunt from a payphone to pick us up. It felt devastatingly late, though it may not have even been midnight.

This was often what it was like when we were all together. Car rides for a family excursion would be abandoned halfway down the street from the house. The car would start turning before anyone could say, "Don't make me turn this car around" and screech into the driveway. Doors yanked open for each family member to pour out in anger. As the youngest, I watched their movements and did my best not to complain or cry. Cries made me a target, and yet, I couldn't stop myself from crying.

In the house, everyone did their best to stay clear of the rest. The teenagers escaped into girlfriends and cars. My dad escaped into projects in his garage becoming nothing but a light the size of a door in the dark. For those of us left—my mother, third eldest brother, and me—TV became our escape. With one in the family room, one in my parents' bedroom, and one in the boys' room, it became easy for the three of us to separate, shut down, and go numb. One of my favorite escapes was *Full House*. "TGIF" felt literal as I waited for the long week to end, so I could spy on a well-kept home with a white family and marvel at the mild tones the adults spoke in and how they got down on a knee to address the children. The children were all girls, chatty, and demanding. No episode went by without one of them complaining or crying, and yet, it was never a problem.

Sometimes I could escape to my cousin's house, which wasn't too dissimilar from *Full House*. For one, she had a white mom, and the house had an order that never existed at mine. The kitchen had an ivy leaf border across the top of the wall and ivy leaf accessories all around to match. They had a living room no one sat in with artifacts from Europe like a giant globe that's top half opened to reveal a bar that no one drank from. In the family room, a big, white fur rug, reminiscent of a bear rug, laid across the floor. After a tidy dinner of chicken breast, baked potato, and broccoli with cheese sauce, we'd move into the living room to watch TV together.

My uncle loved *Hunter*. While the episode played, he and my aunt sat hand-in-hand at the loveseat. My cousin and I splayed across the bear rug. When TV time was done, she and I padded to her bedroom where a queen bed was decorated with an 80s splatter paint bedspread design in pinks and teal with matching pillows and throws. Climbing into bed, my cousin instructed me to pick a book from her nightstand. After TV time was reading time, and then bed. I picked up a fairytale anthology and flipped aimlessly through pages. I didn't know what I was to do with it. I looked over to my cousin and found her eyes focused on the pages in front of her. She seemed to be enjoying herself.

"What are you doing?"

"I'm reading *The Secret Garden*."

"Do you like it?"

"Want me to read it to you?"

"Sure!" And she did. And I curled up next to her like a cat to listen. After a while the books went down, the reading light switched off, and I fell asleep safe and satiated.

In the introduction to *Women Who Run With the Wolves: Myths and Stories of the Wild Woman Archetype*, psychoanalyst and post-trauma specialist, Clarissa

Pinkole Estés, Ph.D. writers, "Stories are medicine. I have been taken with stories since I heard my first. They have such power; they do not require that we do, be, act, anything—we need only listen." I find Estés' words comforting as a writer who has always struggled with reading.

Nearly every professional writer, and every writing teacher, will tell you the best way to improve your writing is to read. Read widely. Read often. Read what you love. Read what inspires you. Read.

Not so long ago, in the pre-Covid times, a well-known writer took to Twitter to pronounce a slightly different interpretation of this rule. They Tweeted something along the lines of, "If you don't love to read, writing is not for you." The declaration was met by a firestorm of clap backs. The writer was confused. How could reading be controversial? In their defense, they Tweeted again saying this was known and commonly accepted advice.

True, and not true.

Advising people to read to become better writers is not the same as saying, if you don't love to read, you shouldn't be a writer. Like me, young learners experience a variety of barriers to becoming proficient readers including, and not limited to, learning difficulties, English as a second language, growing up in a working class or immigrant household, a lack of access to books that speak to personal experience, past trauma, and struggles with mental health.

Not everyone is gifted with joyful introductions to books that allow for a *love* of reading to flourish. For some, reading is a mystery and for others a struggle, but this does not quelch a need for stories.

What if "reading" could look like many things? Listening, communing, watching, walking, dreaming, singing, dancing, acting, even napping, might also be reading. What might that mean for all the burgeoning storytellers waiting for permission to speak? Imagine how much more medicine the world could have.

The Whipping Boy by Sid Fleischman was the first book I read on my own. My third-grade teacher, Ms. Herrera, read it in parts to us over a week. At the end of lunch each day, I'd rush to my desk thrilled to watch Ms. Herrera move to the corner of the blackboard where I knew the book waited to be re-opened.

"Can anyone tell me what's happened in the story so far?" she'd ask, and I'd dart my hand up into the air to retell details from the day before. I had a crush on Ms. Herrera and her late 80s chocolate feathered hair. She wore lavender sweaters that hugged her soft body, and she never yelled or grew angry. My hand was often shot up in the air to catch her attention and bring her my way. "Wow, Xiomara! I love your enthusiasm," she'd say, which made me beam. Reading hour was my favorite part of the day, and when she finished the last page of *The Whipping Boy*, I asked if I could take the book home.

Maybe I asked for the book to keep her beauty close even after I left the classroom.

I finished my reading so quickly that I impressed myself. I didn't know I could read a whole book! Only a couple of days after borrowing the copy, I bound to Ms. Herrera's desk, book in hand, to share my accomplishment.

"Ms. Herrera, I finished it! I read it all on my own!" But when she took the book back, she didn't give her usual encouragement. I immediately shrunk in on myself. Did she think I had cheated since she read it to me first? Did my reading not count? Looking back this may have been my first experience with imposter syndrome.

Jennifer V. Fayard Ph.D. in the article, "Why Rewatching TV Shows Feels So Good," published in *Psychology Today* states, "experiencing something previously increases something called perceptual fluency, or the ease with which we can process information, in subsequent experiences. When something is easy to process, it tends to make us feel positive emotions, which in turn make us like the object more." In other words, by enjoying Ms. Herrera's reading of *The Whipping Boy*, I was able to enjoy the book on my own. My love for Ms. Herrera transferred into positive feelings for reading. It's no wonder that being read to is still one of my favorite acts of love.

By junior high, I started reading more, but only to gain points in the *Book It!* program and the chance to win a free personal-sized pizza. I would read a book for the thrill of being sent to the library to sit at the green-screened Macintosh and take a multiple-choice quiz. Each book test was worth a certain amount of points. The harder the book, the more points you could earn. *Gone with the Wind* was worth the most.

I made it to 75 points, which meant my name was called at assembly. The effort was worth the price of walking up in front of the whole school to receive a blue bookmark that said, "Book It!" across the top. (I don't think I ever made enough points for a pizza.)

In high school, I am proud to say, I completed at least one summer reading assignment. When I saw *The Color Purple* by Alice Walker on the list of books to choose from, I remembered having seen a copy of the VHS back home in our garage. My dad had a video rental shop back in the mid-eighties called "Classic Rentals." That was the premise; they only had the classics. It was one of his many short-lived endeavors, which included a flower shop, burrito stand, and party balloon installations. Now in the 90s, his inventory of VHS tapes lived in stacked boxes in our garage growing dust alongside an old helium tank. On bored summer days, I rummaged through the boxes to see what I could find. This is how I came to watch *A Chorus Line* and how I got a copy of *The Sound of Music*.

I knew *The Color Purple* was in the inventory, so it seemed like the easiest choice. Plus, a copy of the book lived in my eldest brother's small left-behind library from when he moved away to college. *Spy Vs Spy, Calvin and Hobbes, 1984, Malcom X,* and *The Color Purple* were all that remained from his absence. I took my dad's tape and played the first couple of scenes. Next, I flipped open my brother's book, and read just as far. Over days, I continued this process until both the movie and book were done. Knowing what was to happen helped me read, and it was like *The Whipping Boy* all over again.

Even though I still didn't enjoy reading, English was my favorite class. Just as in grade school, in-class reading and book discussions were the best part of my day. Like I'd done so many times before, I enjoyed listening to others read as well as share their retellings of the plot and interpretations. When the teacher would ask, "What do you think the moor symbolizes?" I'd raise my hand, and, taking bits from all I heard, I'd talk about how the moor represented the unknown, the wild parts of her inner self the main character desired to explore, or some such thing as that.

"That's great, Xiomara!" teachers would say. It wasn't uncommon to earn an A on a test for a book I never read as long as I was present and participating.

One of the few books I remember reading for class was *The Handmaid's Tale* by Margarette Atwood. I read it because Ms. Johnson was the first feminist I ever met. One day in class she explained why her name was Ms. and not Mrs. even though she was married. She said, "Because I'm not missing anything, and I don't belong to anyone but me." She was a tall Irish American woman with big, curly red hair. She spoke to us like regular people, and I didn't want to disappoint her. But even she couldn't convince me to read *Wuthering Heights*.

Though we tend to think of reading as a solitary act, it can more often than not be communal. Pinkola Estés, Ph.D., argues that the art of the story "strengthens and arights the individual and the community." The first stories were spoken and shared between the storyteller and the listener. And then they became performances as songs and dramas shared between performers and an audience. We as writers consider our reader as we write. There are relationships in reading, and maybe seeing reading as a communal act could be for the betterment of all.

In college I majored in theatre. Reading plays for class, I enjoyed that their structure meant less words on the page. Plays were faster to read, easier to understand, and could be read within a group with each reader taking on a role. Theory and criticism classes were again my favorites. I loved reading *True West*, *Cat on a Hot Tin Roof*, *Wit*, and *Antigone*. I loved talking about themes, symbols, structure, foil characters, and character motivation. I wrote a paper I was particularly proud of on *True West* and Sam Shepherd's western motif portrayed through foil characters that represented *good* and *bad*. To this day, if I'm trying to write a particularly emotional scene, I bring in elements of the natural environment à la Tennessee Williams' *Cat on a Hot Tin Roof*.

In my voice class, I had an assignment to memorize a Shakespeare sonnet. My teacher, a little Italian woman who had bit parts in many primetime procedurals, taught me how to embody the words. She showed me how to find the places to breathe and how the sounds of the words Shakespeare chose could tell me how the speaker of the piece felt. The soft "ah" sound in the words *awesome* and *heart* was a sound of longing and drew out from the chest. The "r" in words like *roar* and *rage* connoted anger and planted in the core. She taught me that reading could be an act of the body, and it didn't need to be all tied up in the mind. The revelation was thrilling!

But when I entered an MFA program at 27, I felt shamefully inadequate. Others in my cohort had Literature, Creative Writing, and Composition degrees. Others in my cohort had read *Ulysses*, *As I Lay Dying*, *Dante's Inferno*, *Moby Dick*, *The Great Gatsby*. As a poet I felt I was expected to know the complete works of Emily Dickson, Edward Hirsch, and other white poets, most of whom were men.

Someone makes a declaration like, *You have to love reading to be a writer,* and suddenly you have a big, bad secret. You're on borrowed time. One day the reading police will discover you never finished *100 Years of Solitude*, and your WRITER card will be revoked!

The first book of poetry I ever bought and read was *Cotton Candy on a Rainy Day* by Nikki Giovanni. I bought the book because the cute guy I was crushing on in my Acting II class recommended it to me. By then I was probably a college Junior and in my early 20s. What if there is a correlation between the people we love and what we read?

In 2020, the only book I could manage reading was *Book of Delights* by Ross Gay, a collection of flash essays, each one written about one day's "delight." It was the calming, quick read I needed, but even that I never finished. I did, on the other hand, rewatch all seven seasons of *Gilmore Girls* for the 4th time. And I'm not the only one. During the hardest days of Covid, many news sites noted a trend in rewatching favorite TV shows. In "Why Rewatching TV Shows Feels So Good," a 2021 *Psychology Today* article, Jennifer V. Fayard Ph.D. noted that individuals were experiencing a heavier "cognitive load," or amounts of stress. Traversing daily life in lockdowns created so much extra work for our brains that there wasn't much room for new information, and old stories became a balm. Our current world is so chaotic, so filled with pain and violence, why add to it by constituting what reading *should* be.

For some of us reading is hard, and stress caused by a multitude of factors can make it harder. Sometimes it's easier to listen to the audiobook, watch the movie, or even ask a friend what happens, and it's not because we're cheaters, but because it's what our brains can handle. And isn't honoring the needs of our minds and bodies part of the medicine Estés speaks of?

I want to ease your stress. I want to confess my dirty little writer-reader secrets, so you don't have to. Is it helping? Secret telling is scary business, so let me gift you two final stories.

ONE

I was a senior at a Catholic high school. It was not uncommon for me to argue with my religion teacher about gay rights or abortion rights. I was known for speaking up in history class to ask where all the women were in the story.

"The book says 200 men made it to Oregon, but where are the women? I know those men didn't travel alone," I said one time.

"Not again," grumbled a blond jock. The teacher-coach sighed through his mustache and continued on with his lesson as if I said nothing. I also liked to talk about immigrant rights and worker rights. I got a reputation. At least once I can remember being called, "brown power girl."

But then one day at lunch, the newly renovated library had just opened, and I decided to take a look. The room was five times bigger than the previous school library, and there was a wall of windows where I could see my lunch crew sitting just on the other side laughing. I was tired of all the noise and remember thinking how clean and quiet the library felt. I went to the card catalog and sifted through the index cards. I found something of interest and walked through the stacks to find the book that matched the number in my hand. I stopped at a shelf and pulled the book out. The cover was black with the silhouette of four people in red each holding up a fist. In white the words read, *CHICANO!*

I sat cross-legged right in the middle of the aisle and read until a bell rang signaling the end of lunch. It was the first time I felt seen by a book.

TWO

I was in grad school and in my late 20s. Each month, I was tasked with reading three poetry books and writing an annotation (essentially a book report) for each along with 10 new pages of poetry. On days I had a hard time focusing, I drove to my grandmother's house in Boyle Heights with the books.

One afternoon, I knocked on the door, and she let me in. Outside the ice cream truck could be heard playing its usual tin-y *Twinkle Twinkle*. The guy pushing a vending cart bellowed out, "Eloooooooooooteeeeeeee." But inside everything was still and in its place.

"¡Hola Grandma!" I gave her a hug. "Vengo a trabajar."

"Bien. Bien," she said. She knew I didn't speak much Spanish, and I knew she didn't speak any English. Through gestures, we sat down at the family room just beyond the front door. She sat on one couch, and I sat on the other. I took out a poetry book.

"Poemas." I showed the book to her. She took out a prayer book. We read together silently in the afternoon light. Eventually, my eyes grew heavy, (it's what always happens to me when I read), and my head dropped. She handed me a pillow and invited me to lay and rest.

When I woke from my nap, we moved into the kitchen so she could serve me dinner, and then I went home. It was the best reading I ever did.

So sure, being a writer means also being a reader. But does every writer have to *love* reading? Maybe it's enough to love each other, listen to one another's stories, and let the medicine do what the medicine does. I hope you find medicine in these pages.

FRESH SQUEEZED
Ruth Garcia

The orange tree looked beautiful under the pink hues of the setting sun
I know I have to wait for them to ripen
just waiting in hopes that one day they'll be ready
their time will come, I know it
they'll be ready to be loved and cherished by those who pick it
my orange tree is almost there
every sunset is another day closer
whether it's sweet or tart
there will always be a place for them
no matter what
the oranges glow
although there's some bumps and bruises
they are perfect in every way
and when they are ripe
that day will be under the pink sky
it will be the happiest day of my life.

La carreta
Javier Villarreal

Ruedas abultadas que a penas
quebrantan interminables distancias
a vuelta de centímetros y reproches.
Crujen los rayos broncos en el ajetreo.
Amortiguadas al tiempo gimen las redilas.
Lejanas errancias irrumpen silencios
apilados por el tumbo de los años.
Bueyes subyugados bajo las sombras
macilentas de un incesante atardecer.
Sin perder paso el "bueyero"
los llama por su nombre:
¡Vamos, Niño! ¡Vamos, Bonito!
Con la pica espolea su yunta
que avanza ante el manso rumor de la tarde.
Otra voz interrumpe la jornada.
--Hijo, ¿dónde estás?

Bellus et Temporalis Est

(After Morgan Reed's "Paradigm Shifts")

Daniel García Ordaz

and before I could memorize her flawless face,
she faded into spectral blues
faded into ghostly hues,
surfing to and fro within the brilliant, manic crowd—
a speedy purple murmuration—
quick as a painter's stroke,
dancing in the flirtatious rain,
off to catch another train
in the afternoon rushes,
flitting free as artist's brushes,
clinging tightly to her traveling companion—
a pair of souls gleefully lost in the grand abyss
of parasols parasailing in the sisterly bliss
of comings and goings,
of castoffs and moorings,
of eternally effervescent sunset encounters

between vibrantly umbrellaed muses
and innocent bystanders splattered by the slippery drops of love's oblivion

Tu Marea

Fernando Baeza

Si abres tu armario encontrarás un obsequio, como un afecto del sol a la luna. Y quiero empezar con decirte, que ni aun como poeta pudiera decirte todo lo que sale de mi mundo, pero se que tan seguro como el rocío acaricia las flores del campo, así quisieran mis palabras acariciar tu nombre, letra a letra.

Sé que te das cuenta de ser algo diferente contigo, y deveras, por mi vida ni yo lo esperaba. Si supieras como los cruceros se atracan por las aguas del mar, sin deslumbró quisiera contártelo y decírselo a una persona, que he conocido el mundo. Pero caer en tu playa,

y haberte admirado no me doy el derecho a pensar que pudieras soñar con el sol. Y no se tu,

pero el atrevimiento me arrebata el miedo, y tu, podras ser como la gaviota con su inteligencia no se atraba con el viento, y te entregas a tu instinto de mujer? Tal vez no te merezca, tal vez tengas miedo, pero estas manos serán tu escudo y suavecitas contigo como las olas sobre la espuma. Nada me preparó por conocerte, y aun no se como me paso,

pero se que eres mas   eres mas que la luz y el fuego.

Se también, que si ellos te conocieran como yo te viera, mucho más te desearían. Imaginarme como cantas, como ries, y como bailas a luna llena, como cuando caminas por la costa sobre el agua y arena, de pie descalzo y libre como la brisa

que toca tu pelo azabache,

que es mas negro que el obsidiana, pero brilla mas fuerte que un diamante.

Se, que aparento ser enigmático, pero contigo no hay misterio, como libro de vida te dije cosas asi de facil, que nadie alli jamas sabrá.

Encuentro mil excusas para platicar y ver alguna evidencia si tu tambien sufres igual a yo, si por las noches la luna también pensara en alguien, que con ella nos unamos, que nos hablemos, y tal vez sea una propuesta indiscreta pero que fuerza rompe los caprichos del corazon? Y buscar mil excusas para no verte, no voltear a tu lado y veas mi vulnerabilidad. Y te lo juro por Dios, jamás pensé atracarme en tu marea, nunca te vi como aquellos que te han amado, y quisieron invadir tu cuerpo como el calor del sol que invade toda la faz de la tierra.

Alan Kurdi (2012-2015)
Hongwei Bao

like a seabird, wings broken after a heavy thunderstorm
like a sea lion, stranded on a sandy beach
like a sailor, falling asleep after a long voyage
he lay there still
facing the ocean and limbs stretched
wet t-shirt and shorts stuck to the body
colours of red, white and blue

his ears erect, listening to
booming sounds of bombs falling in his home city

FOUR
Ceci M. Valdez

Sky blue snip of yarn
tied around her hair
The clicky-click-clicks of her slick, polished little steps,
Soft percussion down the sidewalk
to Ms. Ebersole's classroom Everything's so scary, so interesting
and
so very new

She doesn't speak
unless it's recess,
In the shade of a Fresno tree she turns into a comedian This tiny chameleon
Last month
she was only three
Now she sings
around the mulberry
and
Her favorite color
is
blue.

WHEN I WAS MADE OF SAND
Dahlia Aguilar

Memory wanders, gulf-bound
waterlogged but not seasick
      never seasick.

             When I was made of sand I dove
             deep to the Gulf floor, searched
                    seashells for signs of life, thought
                          about crab who leaves the calcite castle
                              behind her. People ask me
                                    if I miss Corpus Christi.

                            When I was made of sand, I could
                 hold my breath for a long time. Daddy
          taught me. I won my distance
    ten seconds at a time
ten more seconds and
    ten more seconds.

        Swam several bars from shore,
            forgot my family, pretended:
                I can't hear you, mama. Until

I couldn't. Hear her call
    me back to shore, call
        Daddy back from drink.

           Keep that nickel between your legs. Don't
              get married, ever. I can still hear daddy

            far as I swim

               far as I swim

                  far as I swim.

cafe sira,
may 19, 2024

Heather Cathleen Cox

building pretends she's not old as time, veneered in trendy graffiti, yet
her ancient stone walls whisper to me she wasn't always a dive, plating whitish-green
bricks of Romaine atop blocks of feta, minced tomatoes splattered sparingly, where
hipsters sit adjacent boomers, each tabling their respective rolling papers. tobacco,
weed, whatever.

> melancholy youth in the black trash bag dress orders a soy cappuccino
> from an outside window, carries it into the same beam of Jerusalem sun alighting
> my zipped, avocado green, hemp satchel housing one-eighth of a watermelon,
> a short stack of pita bread, and four cans of oil-packed American Brand tuna.
> *lunches—or dinners.*

guy with a black, rounding moustache and pearling necklace steps toward the table
we're sharing with an elder woman adorned in a turquoise mumu, his hoop silver
earring glistens upon her fork as she rakes it across a greenfree salad. peripherally,
the resident tricolor cat meows for her supper and the walls shout in posters,
Bring Hersch Home.

> distinguishing between large *kippahs* and *taqiyahs* is difficult if they're
> woven of similar materials and the vivid colors blend into the stories this
> coffee alcove cannot disclose. *so…let it be our secret, my foamy chai latte*, laced
> with two espresso shots, an entire stick of cinnamon, the woman I'm
> destined to become.

Dissolving your jobs
Osmani Ochoa

Future is

excited about robots, job automation, cars that drive themselves.

Present-day is

rattled by traversing Mexicans, Haitians, Venezuelans. Two-party dictatorship plans to launch unprecedented border wars,   mass deportations of people   *not*   the billionaires' robots *actually* dissolving your jobs.

On Rilke
William Derge

Don't leave out care.
I cared enough to
save the desk's veneer.
So, I put my coffee
on a few Sonnets
to Orpheus
The result: a pair
of interlocking circles,
brown rings that
a myopic rider
on a carousel grabs for
but never quite fully grasps,
or those that hang for
the gymnast's rosined hands.
She raises herself up,
and then, to affect
a final spin in the air,
she lets go,
leaving us wondering
where and how
she'll ever land,
or even if.

400 DAYS
David Ndubuisi

It's been months since i gained "freedom" from my parents
and could I say something changed?
If it's the way I see the world or
the way life scratched the festering wounds
on my back, yes I would say something changed.
For the first time, I opened my eyes to see, not usually from my mother's lens,
the first time I fell without support from my dad,
and it was the first time I blinded myself with shards of earthly glass.
I believe I may have changed or changed things that shouldn't have changed
but I'll probably never know till I'm too late since my parents
aren't here to point out the road in the darkness.

Canto funesto para Elsbeth Bathory

Iván Medina Castro

Pálida la luna de tu carne
que agresiva transparenta
el azul voraz de tus venas.
Leche y sangre es tu rostro,
silencio aterrador:
sin suspiros, aliento o palpitación.
Estatua marmórea
de negra cabellera como ala de cuervo
cubre tus senos pergaminos.
¡Oh belleza húngara
de labios escarlata
y grandes ojos oscuros!
Alma mía,
vuelve, vuelve del abismo ignoto
y recorramos juntos el sendero
ruta a nuestro jardín
que ya no comparten tus ojos.
Romántica agonía,
me niego a dejarte
en esta fría y mefítica prisión
y haciendo caso a la lasciva de mi alma,
te tomaré una y otra vez
hasta que la rigidez de tu cuerpo me lo prohíba.

Abraxas

Iván Medina Castro

Sedante, cual mártir herido
fue tu quejido armonioso
lúdica maldita;
con gemidos placenteros
a caudales incestuosos.
Negra reina,
realeza plétora,
Zingua angoleña.
Cercena al adamita caído
que se detiene
agotado, jadeante y flácido.
Y al velo de ideas oscuras
suelta el soplido
de gritos resonantes
desde el diapasón de tu cólera
para estremecer la cadencia de la selva
por la insatisfacción y la pena.

Changüí
Iván Medina Castro

Campesino de piel curtida
por el aire de esta vida,
 pregona a la tierra,
 a tu Cecilia guajira.
Ara a la madre labriego
 fecundando su interior
con azadón, semilla y sudor.
Pizca el fruto de tu entrega,
con alegría; canto que llega.
Campestre beodo
por el néctar de la caña
del hijo de tu entraña,
 sin bohío, pero esperanza.
Pulula libre por el monte guajiro,
entre la trémula mata ciguaraya
que exhala el verano
 donde el aire invisible es puro y claro.
Contempla la quietud
 del árbol que se eleva
con magnífico esplendor
en este tupido jardín
donde quema el brusco sol
 que es la Sierra Maestra.

Opposing View
Barbara Gurney

Emotions strong
Heart beat rising
Sweat on brow
Placards held high

We need these folk of conviction
These people with challenging views

There'd be no vote for women
No say in what they felt
There'd be no sootless workplace
No fairness on the factory floor

There'd be no bus or trains or planes
If inventions were ignored
There'd be no medical advancement
If defiant risks went unheeded

Emotions strong
Heart beat rising
Sweat on brow
Forging forward

We need these folks of conviction
These people with different views from ours

November 2005

Before the Wall

Falcon Reservoir and Wildlife Refuge

Crischelle Navalta

Over there the land
is just like here.
The ground made of the
same sand, the same minerals,
the same crystals
and fossilized rocks.

Over there the trees grow
            the same.
Low and thin, with
            slender leaves
                    like olive trees,
flashing silver.

Across the imaginary,
invisible boundary across
the reservoir

the water mingles – mingles
with the waves from the South
            lapping northwards
                    and vice versa.

And having divided this
sameness between two countries,
the only differences are
                            names.

孤木春祷

Su Yun

仿佛我擎掌祈祷
祈祷沟壑的底端传出歌谣
仿佛我为歌谣思考
思考这酝酿一冬的曲调
穿过田坳洗脱成符号
神圣地织染形貌
形成流入人间的青藻
寻求牵依的怀抱
终舒展为岭上的枝草
我不息祈祷
直到夕阳漫流环绕
我注目指尖的芽角
这无瑕却渺小
用年轮与枯皱轻褓
感叹道
青春呵，人间最美好的诉告

Spring Prayer of the Lone Tree
Su Yun

As though my palms alone could pray,
Praying for songs to rise from the depths of gorges,
As if I ponder for these songs,
Contemplating the tune,
simmered all winter,
Traversing the fields,
cleansed into symbols sacred,
Dyed and woven into divine forms, Becoming algae that flows into the mortal world,
Seeking a cradle of warmth to clingFinally stretching into the grass on the ridges,
I pray ceaselessly,
Until the evening sun encircles in a golden flood,
 I fix my gaze on the budding tips of my fingers,
 Immaculate yet so faint,
 Swaddled in the rings of years and withered wrinkles,
I sigh,
Oh youth, the most beautiful lament of humanity.

Love is Fickle
Lilia K. Garza

As the flames began to hasten and the matchstick took hold,

Verdant strands began to burst from the sunken hull

And while the gust carried the heaviness of this hell bound path,

Thawing of the arteries kept the heart not quite intact

While crimson flooded the streets of the cities and left nothing aside,

The nation's president could not conceive why

There was such concern for this affair, everyone in a ruckus shared

For what made the residents so scared?

Upon gazing outside, she finally concluded why

The lemon drop yields long since raced past,

The frequency of emotion revolving around an axis

The frigidness of lonely existence no longer in practice

But why now, the spirit shrieks, does this occur?

How have the strands of light reached past the event horizon?

Couldn't you see, the spirit wails, that this was necessary long ago?

But there was no answer, the void showed

And as she smiled at her screen,

The rush of it all began to stream

Out into the open for all to see,

Thus the woman uttered, "I am in love, with her?"

And if I love her, is it because I'm heading into the darkness?

Is she the shortcut through the tunnel?

For rather than fall into the bottomless pit,

I would much rather end on a chapter like this.

Why do I write?

Victoria Montes

Why do I write?
I am human, I see poetry in the most beautiful music.
The emotions that fire painters and potters
Fire my pen to give voice to the emotions that inspire
The most well known artists.
The dreams that drove Vivaldi to hear the four seasons.
Da Vinci captured the mysterious smile of Mona Lisa
This is the legacy that is passed down
to me, that I have inherited. Poets and
writers capture with words the events
of life
That inspires dreams and love and
laughter and joy and sadness. They
capture every big event of life:
marriages, engagements, First dates,
proposals, births, deaths, graduations.
When people fall in love and everything in between.
We are there when families start,
and when babies are born. When
babies grow to children, children
to teenagers
Teenagers to young adults, when those young adults
Go on to start their own families. Writers are
there for everything. The generations that came
before us worked as hard as they did Because they
wanted to lay the foundation for their children and
grandchildren. For something better, they sacrificed
and worked hard because they dreamed. They
dreamed for their children and their grandchildren
To go out into the world and record the beauty and joy
The loss, the pain of everyday
moments, to be the ones who
Brought love and light and hope
and beauty to the world.

Slither
Analyssa Beltran

This envious wrath coils itself around
My mind, squeezing, while seething at the teeth.
Smooth green scales are the façade of the beast
My anger and hate it wears as its crown.
Slithering over my eyes making me
Blind to the suffering I have invoked,
Tighter it squeezes its hold on my throat
Choking out my last few breaths of defeat.
Perhaps I should not have wandered within
The dark jungles where the green snakes reside.
I should have been content to hear your lies
Instead I have poisoned myself with sin.
Fading into the morning and its mist
Ignorance abandons me and my bliss.

The Light I Long For
Joel Hinojosa

To breathe,
I need to be my sacrifice.

My most joyous, bright prose
Is born as I feel myself drowning.

My body is too limited by itself,
So the flood rushes down my face
And onto the ground, filling the room.

Through my tired gaze
And weary arms,
I part that sea
And search for light,
Only to let out one final sigh.

I soon discover—
Only I can make the light I long for.

EL CANTO DEL COYOTE Y EL SOL

Demian Palacios

El tiempo se llevó al sol
con el canto de los años tristes,
ya no caen plumas en el aire.

Donde todo se hacía lluvia,
un colibrí de madera que se hace nube
y la diosa luna carga un conejo de noche.

Los días se mueven en piedras bajo el agua,
la vida nace con las primeras formas,
que surgen en las hojas verdes
y las hojas amarillas que tienen las tardes del sol.

El camino de las estrellas pasa con el canto
de la piedra blanca,
las palmas sonando con el canto verde
de un quetzal.

En este cerro de los astros
un coyote escupe al sol,
y el sol a la tormenta de la luna
y el centro de flores cubrirá el pantano.

Sobre las piedras se levantan las nubes
que van de una montaña al mar,
dentro de la peña viven los muertos
y los seres nacen semilla.
Para que el viento nos acerque
agua del cielo,
será mejor un canto de noche,
un aposento y un ave que cante
con la voz de las flores.

A SIETE DÍAS SE OCULTA EL SOL

Demian Palacios

Cedan los terrenos del agua
o los suelos santos,
suras de una meca
certezas de dichos de Muhámmad

Él hizo salir de sus hogares
la aleya de la usura y del hambre;
traerá la guerra de Alá,
a siete días donde se oculta el sol.

Hashem espera que caigan las mezquitas,
vuelve con malas artes al mundo en la ceniza,
el silencio se escucha en el valle del Nilo
con apelaciones de muertos sin nombre.

Él es el eterno que vuela sobre los cuerpos,
y otros piden refugio por debajo de la arena;
venimos al paso de los reyes a Jerusalén
peregrinando estrellas del cielo.

Ya no huele,
ni saben como antes el falafel y el hamin,
con voz tranquila, se repite el llanto
que han puesto las noches sobre la luz.

Nos han guiado a este lugar sin rumbo
los mensajeros no trajeron la verdad:
solo querían restos en las cruces,
nos hicieron de barro
nuestra claridad se va en la luz del alba.

Flox rabiosa
Joselin Mejía

Te tiendes sobre cada página no escrita
en el bosque de la memoria,
encuentras esa palabra estrepitosa
que el ojo anhela.

Expulsas el lenguaje de tu cuerpo
y con ello, los muertos, luego respiras
y te das cuenta que tu idioma
está hecho de huertos,
de gaviotas, de patíbulos.

Había una fábula en la tirada de dados,
un nombre de labios carmesí,
después se hizo un árbol en tu cabeza,
un enjambre, una bandera amiga,
una bandera enemiga, una voz tupida.

Tuviste que romper las sílabas,
labrar un páramo, hacerte nómada,
aprender que las heridas
también se leen en braille.

Que no sanan en 40 días,
que se vuelven guetos en las gargantas,
mira allí donde está clavada el hacha.
he ahí el signo, he ahí la oración.

Hay cosas que no pasan
Joselin Mejía

Mi padre nunca pudo ser mi padre
porque él no tuvo uno
eso era lo que decía.

Tenía 5 años cuando lo conoció
y el viejo dudó
que fuera su hijo.

De ahí esa palabra
ajena y extraña,
esa semilla vacía.

Hay cosas que no pasan,
nunca jugó conmigo
porque le recordaba a su infancia

pero de grande me dijo:
- cuídate de los lobos -,
ahora sé que se refería a los hombres.

Jamás pasó por mí a la escuela,
pero me regaló una libreta empastada,
tenía mi pseudónimo de escritora.

No viajamos juntos,
pero pagó todas mis clases de inglés
para que pudiera entender la poesía de Keats.

Él admiraba a César,
pero nunca habló de Bruto,
desconocía que su hijo predilecto
le había clavado la última puñalada.

No quería hablar de mi padre
porque siempre encontré
más ausencias que virtudes
y hoy estoy aquí,
haciendo un poema para él.

Rostro

Arthur Haneke

Viendo el resplandor de tu belleza
Qué contempla tu hermosura
Acompañada de tu naturaleza
Y frescura

Es tu rostro que me deja atónito
Callado y distraído
Dejando mis ojos ciegos
 Y mi cuerpo apagado

Francamente no sé si esto será arte
 Oh no si es arte, oh no se si es arte
Pero no puedo negar que es lo
Más resplandeciente que jamás
Haya visto
Oh resplandeciente, oh resplandeciente

Pajarito
Arthur Haneke

¡Ámame, pajarito lindo!
Que hay mariposas
Hermosas en mi garganta
Y que por eso te dedico
Está romantica prosa
Que necesitas
 Que la sonrisa de tu boca
Roce ese sentimiento que llevo dentro
Que me tiene ardiendo
Con ternura y sin sosiego
¡Ámame, pajarito lindo!

(sin título)
Arthur Haneke

Existencia
  Tu amor es el pincel
 Que le da color a mi vida
Tus abrazos y besos
Hacen que mis sentimientos
Sean mas hermosos
Y cariñosos

Mi existencia te lo debo a ti, amor
Ni las lluvias más torrenciales
Ni los 7 pecados capitales
Podrá destruir esta
Está relación frutifera

Nuestra lucha es
Contra nuestro propios males
Ganeremos, oh si ganaremos
Armonía agradulce: cantos de los pajaritos
Es vida, es melodía
 Cerca de ti, me vuelvo cada vez más feliz

Opuka
Clara Elena García

La yvy
Opuka
Ha che
Ahendu

La yvytu
Opuka
Ha che
Ahecha

La ysyry
Opuka
Ha che
Aguata

Che sy
Opuka
Ha che
Añe'ê

La tierra
Se ríe
Y yo
Escucho

La montaña
Se ríe
Y yo
Veo

La rivera
Se ríe
Y yo
Camino

Mi madre
Se ríe
Y yo
Hablo

The earth
Laughs
And I
Listen

The mountain
Laughs
And I
Observe

The brook
Laughs
And I
Walk

My mother
Laughs
And I
Speak

Snow As You
Naomi Alegre

The chaos thrown at me is less here.

We go back in circles sometimes, my mind and I, never once reaching our destination.

 For me to peel back the outer layer & allow myself to breathe.

What was breathing again?

Dark. Moody. Misunderstood.

She is running away from everything she knows, never once reaching her destination.

The refuge I find is in knowing.

I cannot control all the versions of me that exist in other people's minds.

To do that would be impossible.

So, I hide.

Not in a closet but between black and white white white space.

Wishing it was snow as you.

The Poet and The Gardner

Líza Rivera

The Poet
Like the Gardner
Learns to pay close attention
To the world around them

To appreciate beauty
For beauty's sake
To nurture
Life's smallest seed

They revere
Each dainty leaf
Listen closely
To the whispers of the wild

Hold the universe
In the palm of their hand
And see the Divine
In everything

Both the Poet
And the Gardner
Live to share their bounty
With us all

Rivers of My Life

--a paean to the Rio Grande Valley

Feroza Jussawalla

Mestizaje

Kaveri and Godavari flow through my veins,
Ganga, Jamuna I have never seen,
though I have sung about them
many times. They say that, their names,
along with that of my motherland,
echo in the hills of the
Vindhyas and Himalayas.

But I have made,
the banks of the Rio Grande,
my home. The land of the dry
salt cedar, juniper, mesquite,
las alturas.

The land of turquoise silversmiths
plateros, whose work,
echoes my name,
as they
pull turquoise from
the Kingman mines,
to crown their rings
and squash blossoms.

Here I have found my home,
in my metaphorical mestizaje. Adopted
though not conceived in, the salty soil
of the banks of the Rio Grande,
Tejano, Nuevo Mexico,
pero soy de la India...
but we are all Indians, Indios...
ALL.

Palpita la luz...
Seudónimo: Chaneque.

Palpita la luz del entendimiento.
Una idea. Una palabra. Luego otra.

Después de un latido luminoso
se entreabren las estrellas.

Se reúnen días y siglos de la voz humana.
Tormento y agonía.

El hombre escribe su poesía
con la alegría del panadero
que hace milagros con sus manos.

La poesía se vuelve cereal,
tierra, arena, mujer, dioses, viento.

Toma su pluma y con tinta clorofílica
empieza a tatuar el dorso del papel,
que gusta ver su piel colmada de letras.

La idea es una torre ardiente,
colmena de una líquida miel de oro,
cristalina y deslumbrante
para la tierra fértil e invencible de la memoria.

Se van agrupando los versos
que son como campos de trigo o de sorgo
que sonrientes anuncian
la victoria de la germinación en su cuerpo.

Se detiene la mano. Ya nadie dicta la obra:
se dispuso la última palabra.

Con fulgor de enredadera y metales
se bautiza al poema
después de la travesía
sobre la cordillera providencial
o tortuosa de la mente.

Germina el grano…

Germina el grano de luz.
Cereal buscando en la oscuridad de la memoria.

Ni monje ni templo te ayudan
en el calvario a solas de la palabra.

Permanece sonora la idea.

Viento victorioso de letras
que brotan del manantial alegre
del vientre de la tierra.

Reina una alegría de pescadores
al poner punto final al poema.

Motionless and Visible like a Great Sorrow
After Pablo Neruda

Laura Peña

I've gone back again to the lonely bedrooms
How much of the darkness in my soul
Would I give to regain you

Nothing's left today
Except my flimsy skeleton
My eyes unhinged

Until all is transparent
There under the earth
And my sleep can be tranquil

It was beautiful
To have lived
When you lived

The drowned arm, uplifting
Carries the kiss of the salt
In a droplet

A Marine Yearns for Morphine

J. Villanueva

Down in the stumps, you said it wasn't
A big deal—a knee almost twisting
Out of socket. A current rising in the unfamiliar.

On a rare rainy day, 29 Palms
Felt like Atlantis. We ran to the smoke pit
From the corner store. 2 lost souls. Cold
Beer in each hand from the torn cardboard

Box from which we shared. Like Valhalla
Here on earth except rain here is barely that. And I
don't feel like much of a warrior
When the pain is creeping
Its way back—

And I don't think I'll ever be completely whole

Anymore. When so much of my brain is broken. And I feel like I need it to get
through my day—

Any more and I probably won't be able to breathe, Won't be able to taste the
next Coors I open.

I've grown accustomed to my friends' blurry faces. Backdrops of old land knowing

That moments of clarity are glimpses
Into the afterlife. And it's too scary

To face alone.

The dealer leans into my window for a quick handshake. I find myself speeding
away back to my current life—
Back to delirium and unfettered movement. How happy I am when I
least like myself.

How beautiful the Mojave is in its mists. How perfect the sands look for
self-interment.

Squeezing the World to Our Will
Kathy Trenfield Raines

Grackles, seagulls, starlings and house sparrows,
Brown anoles (not green) and fox squirrels,
Coyotes, raccoons and bobcats (nothing against these fellows)—
Creatures, like us, who'll eat about anything,
May be all the company we have left
As choosier creatures fly, crawl, slither or swim away—
Or die.

We mangle and manicure forests, waters and savannahs,
We slice and sort them into cleanly shaven yards and lots.
We yank out ebonies, huisaches, yucca, sabal palms
And replace with oaks, chinaberries and Washingtonia palms
Trees foreign and unappealing to native creatures,
And sometimes completely ignored,
Making our world lonelier.

For what?
For trinkets, endless clothing,
Constant connection,
Big TVs, massive trucks.

Nguyen
PW Covington

Nguyen was my friend in prison
Nguyen was a baker

Nguyen was 5 years older than me
I was born in 1974

Nguyen had been flown out of South Vietnam
As a toddler, by the US Air Force

Nguyen owned a bakery and had sent two kids to college

Nguyen killed his wife and her lover
Nguyen pled to consecutive life
Ngyuen was to be deported
Sometime soon
Criminal Alien

Nguyen had attorneys, trying to fight it
Would rather die old in a Texas prison

Nguyen baked in the prison kitchen
Midnights spent kneading dough, cutting biscuits

Nguyen wept, sometimes, as he told me
How much it hurt him
To not be allowed to use yeast

All powder
Nguyen would say
All powder, no love for baking
No love for baking

I was a baker
Nguyen would say

One night before falling out for work
Nguyen and his boxes of legal documents
Were taken away by US Marshalls

I never saw Nguyen again

It's Not Easy
Michael Gerleman

Have you noticed how hard it is to be good?
For forty days I have gone to the Progresso bridge.
Walking up concrete inclines
pulling wagons with granola bars, soap, ice, water, milk, clothes, sanitary pads,
and once, as a special request, a brown paper bag with condoms.
All for migrants who wait, sleep, eat, and sweat
on a bridge turned into a prison
where people wait to cross those few sacred feet
into a land they believe in
more than I.

I sweat like a cold beer
on a hot humid day, and
my Spanish is a shy toad
hiding under a rock.
Why am I doing this
I wonder? There are others
who speak the language,
who are in better shape,
about whom the men will
not whisper "maricón" even
as they take my food and water.

I'm doing it because no one else is.
I'm doing it because just posting
on social media is not enough.

I'm doing it because they are human.
I'm doing it so one day in the future,
I can say,
"I resisted."

Rhododendrons
Julie Brandon

I have this sound I make, deep in my throat
unbidden, unplanned, unintentional
when it's hot
or humid
or I'm just plan disgusted
something between a yuck and ugh
a bit guttural
today was such a day
As I was leaving a store and stepped into the sticky heat
I made the sound
A woman walking by smiled and said,
"It would be great if we were rhododendrons"
It puzzled me, not being a gardener
and I wondered if she was right
but not having the choice, I turned the a/c on high
leaving the humidity to the rhododendrons
I hope they enjoy it

My Heart is With You
Featured Poet: Trier Ward

This is your first letter
but it won't be the last.
I'm going to write you
every day while you are away.
I put money on your commissary
for envelopes and stamps
so you can write me back.
Every day at three o'clock
I'll be waiting for the mailman.
And every time they let you
have 5 minutes for a phone call,
I'll be the one on the other end
of the line telling you it's okay-
even though 5 minutes is really
only enough time to say hello,
I love you, and goodbye.
Please don't be sad.
My heart is in there with you
and your name is on my lips
each night as I pray for your safety.
Those high walls, those fences
can't keep my love from you.
This heart will never see
a criminal or a delinquent in you-
only a person who deserves
 a second chance,
who I know can do better,
who is beautiful to me.
So hold on to this letter.
Hold on to my love.
We'll be together again soon.

Iron
Featured Poet: Trier Ward

In the Sandia foothills,
sunny and hot,
a fawn-colored bird alit
on a rock jutting out
against the blue sky
near where we had
climbed together with
our family. Our nine
year-old son and
seven-year-old twins
braving the climb
through cacti and
sand slides to
smile at the top.
As the bird flew
off into the desert
sky, I noticed
the stone was bleeding.
I took a drop
of blood from the
stone and tasted it
as I looked at your
proud face staring
off into the Albuquerque landscape.
Then we climbed back down.
And the blood dried in my mouth.
Just a taste of iron.

The Rainbow
Featured Poet: Trier Ward

A rainbow stretches
across Central Avenue
with its fresh grasp
of raw sky
bouncing off the
hard concrete.
Deep hues promising
hope even when life
seems as foreboding
as the thunder,
a question mark.
This mystic arc
emerges from the
sunshine and says
don't give up,
look for my pot of gold
though I have no end,
for I am a wonder to behold
a rare prism,
a newly revealed
wonder of light
bending my body
to show you that
life can still
be beautiful
even when rain
comes down hard.

The Beat Of Life
Luis Trevino

It all started that night.
The day her presence sparked the beat of life.
Step after step,
      dress' swayed,
      boots tapped,
      hair gilded,
      spinning and twirling,
      sweat flew.
We all saw it crisp and clear.
The artful spirit of the dance floor.
Like a marionette hovering over all of them,
      controlling the course of every individual.
Every person having their own rhythmic flow.
Each person moving quickly and majestically,
      everyone, aware of every individual around them.
Time being counted,
      by our claps,
      by our chants.
      by our hearts.
      a rhythmic symphony reaching the heavens.
Reality was paused,
No one cared about the hour.
Children slept on their chairs.
Parents battled on the dance floor.
Never caring about the outside world,
      for the eyes in front of them is all that matters.
She was there, and we all felt it.
It all started that night.

Aurimar in America
Belén Thérèse Garza Flores

Goodbyes smiled in Venezuelan springtime,
birthday party bubbled sweetly
by the Suchiate River. Tender
calls of quetzals, choirs of
white nun orchids. I sang
along to the love songs of
many countries. And I passed
through, hopeful and given.
Mamí, we're out of the jungle.

Driving down a Dallas boulevard,
blue jeans with a
pink BIC lighter and
$8.18. Could this
land of the free be
mine?
In the late October air, my raised hands waved.

So, I suppose this land was
made for you and me, for
taking. I was handed out like
bread to the people.

In a wide, stark field
among strangers in
Texas, my heart no
longer a solid, tangible
form,
my body the whirling stanzas of a lullaby
for those who dream but cannot sleep.

Compline
Charles Darnell

Is it the end of day
or days?
Heat lasts into morning,
rises with the sun.
Breeze blows hot
like billows.
Dante need not look
far for the next ring
of Hell.

Even sunflowers dread
the peek of pink
along the horizon.
Vegetation droops by
mid-morning.
By evening, they lift
rough leaves in prayer for rain.

And we are a clever species,
we tell ourselves we
will adapt, we will find
a way.
No need to raise our
arms in supplication
to an indifferent god.
We did this,we can undo.

I am not sure.

At the end of day,
I pray, not to any god,
but to all living things,
not for renewal,

for forgiveness.

Listen To My Whispers
Vito del Valle

No soul can hear my whispers as the shadows leave me
    moving closer to the center of town
Smelling the sweat of innocent fetuses
    as they play cops and robbers at city park
Calico furred knaves with patching mange
    smirk at the slow Cha-Cha of the shadows
        knowing they'll never reach their prey
My instinct is to collapse, shrivel up
    into a ball of used Christmas tinsel
Abandoned by the black silhouettes that I hold
    so dear against my breast, I die inside
        a thousand deaths in a thousand ways
Who will listen to my murmur? Who will
    help me keep its pulse, its timbre?
The brown skinned heathens of this South Texas
    border town have no use for the mumbling
        of ancient epithets concurring the use of
            love as a weapon by the weak and hopeless
I stand beside myself, ask myself for a cigarette
    but at 10 dollars a pack I'm not inclined to share
Besides we don't have any matches or flint
    or two sticks to rub together, I look at the time
        and wonder when will the shadows return
There are only so many Goddamn embryos in this town
    to devour, the unborn yolks may already be gone
        sitting heavy in some other darkness' pit
They'll find nothing but an empty parking lot and
    they'll come back home, back to me and
        my enduring arms, having no choice
            but to listen to my whispers.

Please, God let me become a tree
Joann González

Please, God
let me become a tree.
So that I may grow and plant seeds (make
volcanoes). Let me be the wind one day
part of the sky that looks on forward.
So that I can inspire
the way they've inspired me.
When my time comes
I will go back to the soil (soul).
Until then,
nourish me with your magic
so that one day I may become a grand tree with plentiful
knowledge ready to whisper it onto many living things.
God,
bless me and my kin.
Thank you,
amen.

Hecho trizas
Érika Garza Tamez

Al ver mi libro hecho trizas
mi corazón también se rompió en mil pedazos,
añicos de azúcar que se volvieron sal y cenizas.

Como si Jack el destripador
hubiera mutilado mi cuerpo
y me hubiera sacado las entrañas sin pudor.

Como a una Coatlicue descuartizada
cubierta en sangre escarlata,
como rompecabezas, literalmente desmembrada.

Quisiera borrar esa imagen de mi mente
pero sigue ahí,
tal vez porque es reciente.

Mis ojos y nariz son sensibles al recuerdo
lo enterraré
como se entierran los muertos.

Torn into shreds
Érika Garza Tamez

When I looked at my book torn into shreds
my heart also broke into a thousand pieces,
smithereens of sugar that turned into salt and ashes.

As if Jack the Ripper
would have mutilated my body
and he would have shamelessly taken out my insides.

Like a dismembered Coatlicue
covered in scarlet blood,
like a puzzle, literally dismembered.

I would like to erase that image from my mind,
but it's still there,
maybe because it's recent.

My eyes and nose are sensitive to this memory,
I will bury it like the dead are buried.

Obscuridad en la luz
Rosalva Ruiz

Llegas sin previo aviso. Esa hermosura de tu desgracia,
sombra larga y azabache, me distrae de mi meta.
Seguido de ese toque lento, mueca de tu quebrantado ego.

Quiero abrazarte, pero me contengo por miedo.
Miedo a lo incontrolable.
De que al tocar ese diente de león se esparza entre el viento,
sin dejar nada, más que desconsuelo.
Miedo de que tus abrazos sean filosos e hirientes.
O de que tus palabras, armas cargadas de furor incesante,
me hieran en este silencio pausante.

No te quiero hacer daño. O tal vez, no me quiero hacer daño.
Puedo romper tu barrera, más no sé si pueda sacarte de ella.

Inclusive tengo miedo de lo que está detrás.
Y si es veneno que achispa esas cenizas.
Esas, que previamente fueron un corazón inocente.
Que ni lágrimas, ni el ahogo ensangrentado
pudieron apagar a ese fuego griego que consumió
mi nave, mi navegante, mi fuerza interna.

Miedo, de esa ave fénix que espera en el limbo su nuevo despertar.
Fénix ardiente y sin sombra que arrasa con todo lo que en mi aflora.

Dime, si te doy la mano, ¿Me seguirías?
¿O, me arrastrarías a tu guarida abismal?

Siento la frialdad y el temblor en tus manos
al ir quitando mi vestimenta de acero.
Estás igual de nerviosa que yo.
Pieza por pieza retumba al caer al suelo.
Cada eco extirpa mi razón de ser.
Me quita las fuerzas y salen mis deseos internos.
No lo puedo negar. Me estremecí al sentirme desnuda frente a ti,
mi otro yo.

Horizontes
Rosalva Ruiz

Bienaventurado, llegado del horizonte, apenado, nervioso y con cautela.
Te creí adorable.

Cuando escuche tu voz,   *en aquella costa*
me enamoré y yo Nausicaa   *te di vida*
Al escuchar tus travesías   *te admiré por tus proezas*
Me emocioné   *y sentí que era parte de ellas.*

Hermosa puesta de sol que ilumina tus hilos sin agarre.
Igual que nuestros tangentes hilos del destino.
Imposible tocarte o tenerte entre mis brazos.

Como a una madre, me diste tu mano. Como amiga, me abriste tu corazón.
Y como a una hija, me diste tu adiós. Pareciera que todo fue una ilusión.

¿Fuiste un sueño?   *¿O fuiste realidad?*
Nuestro encuentro,   *lo recuerdo bien.*
Tú siendo celestial,   *hermoso, cauteloso*
Y yo con falta de amor,   *tu humildad y sabiduría,*
Imaginé, serías mi futuro,   *más todo es un recuerdo.*

Hoy en camino a mis nupcias, me abrazan tus recuerdos.
Nerviosa, veo mi futuro…

¡Morfeo, no te burles! ¡NO, de mí!

Mi horizonte lejano,	*elixir que tanto extrañé,*
por fin estás aquí,	*pero*
Mi Odiseo	*no eres tú.*
Como el aire a la montaña	*ese amor*
es presente,	*una vez más lo sentí,*
Más es invisible	*hacia ti.*

Como rama del árbol, sus ojos se parecen a ti.

Más su humildad, su juventud, su sonrisa nerviosa… Todo, es diferente.

Alcé mi mano y acaricié sus hilos los cuales se aferran a mi agarre.
Los cuales me tientan, me acarician, me desbordan. Soy mujer.

Su mujer

Hoy por fin, puedo ver un nuevo horizonte.

NO TITLE 42,409 DEAD AS OF 16 OCTOBER
2024 (after Godspeed You! Black Emperor)
Max Tyrone Lozano

from our river to your river to our gulf

      to the sea the sea the sea;

our rivers collide & form

      the double-helix of our erasure—

    hide here curved 'round the spikes of the nopal, like my people do.
i can tuck you into the leaf of a tamal

where we buried Amá, where

i found the bones of your ancestors, too.

hide 'neath the shame of being an american, hide here 'neath the torn
vestiges of the west.

your Keffiyeh comforts me at the quince,

as i do the huapango in the dance halls

      of another occupied territory.

bury your mothers alongside my father,

      your children under every flower

         of this scalped border,

      under Cacamatzin's skeleton wig.
i think:

where is your head, America? surely not swept beneath the rug of rubble, under the carpet bomb.

does your father hold your torso

      as your head is laundered

& your limbs contract against themselves? the heart threshes
about the tangle.
no sound from the burning room,

      i think.

        hide here

in greater mexico & lesser america. travel through this
poem,
      my Gaza-Rio Grande vortex.

bring the seeds of olive trees,

plant them here in Ginsberg's beard, so that when they
shoot
      & bear the fruit of a survived race,

your children may carve into them

      & get confused for mexican.

hide here & be seen.

pour from your parched lips
to my ears your stories,

so that we may no longer

      speak solely to walls,

but to our twin narratives—

our rivers that rejoin & form

      the double-helix of our existence.

Güero
Nianna E. Gustovich

Child of mine,
Fetal heart,
I nourish you
With the agave
While the alacrán
Awaits to steal
You from me.
You are fairer
Than the nieve
And glisten next to mi piel morena.
You are loved
Even though you are born
From a distant padre
Who knows not my ways,
An honorable man
Among ladrones,
A man of the West,
No stranger to violence,
Fuerte en creencia,
Though it be not mine.
I cradle you where
The nopal grows,
To protect you
From the beating cascos
Of los otros who
Want to take you from me.
Plantas rodadoras
Bring the dust.
Save us both
Until Salvador comes home.

Mi rifle .22

J. Villarreal

Güelito, aún mantengo
el .22 que me compraste
cuando cumplí 12 años
allá en el rancho.
Fuimos a campear ese día.
Tú, con una escopeta recargada
al hombro, yo con el .22 cargado
de hombría bajo el brazo.
Tus consejos como aves
iban y venían por el monte.
Algunas se colgaban en el aire
volando al compás de mis pasos
hasta que tronaron los primeros disparos.
Mezquites, huizaches y nopales
aún conservan cicatrices como
mudos testigos de mi hombría.
Se cansa la tarde y el sol
se tumba en la distancia.
En su vaivén, el viento
sacude los favores del recuerdo.
La nostalgia se desborda
en esos días de ayer.Acá, en la ciudad, Güelito,
el .22 cargado de añoranza
apunta hacia nuestros días.
Cuando lo desenfundo
escucho el eco de tu voz.
Lo tomo entre las manos
y niño me siento otra vez.
Me arrastra el pensamiento
y te aprecio junto a mí,
susurrándome al oído
--Aquí estoy…
--Aquí estoy, hijo,
sigo junto a ti.

I Walk Around with Invisible Holes

Linda Feliciana Romero

I walk around with invisible holes,
the weight of loss felt with each step

one footin front of the other
      then the other

I.   It's the night of a poetry reading,
        only ten days after
        My friend from out of town
        will surely bring back my smile

        I pretend everything over a cup of shrimp
        My soul is deafened
            to laughter
            to conversation toward me
            to the invitation to stand on stage and read
      except,
            to the fading hiss of my extinguished flame

I walk around with invisible holes,
the weight of loss felt with each step

II.   It's the first Father's Day,
        in Austin for two weeks

        An offer for a lunch gathering
        cues the familiar tightrope,
            my need to be alone,
            without offending
      In vain, trapped,
            morose pleas

        My soul is deafened
            to laughter
            to conversation toward me
      Today,
            there is no mourning silent

Inteligencia artificial
Rogelio de Jesús Cisneros

Hoy leí mayormente
soledad en el pronóstico
del clima. Tengo una aplicación para estos días.

Indicaciones: cierre los ojos y continúe durmiendo. Recuerde: cuatro segundos
para inhalar, cuatro segundos para sostener y seis segundos para exhalar. Cree
una imagen mientras respira.

Escogí transitar por un pasillo, para encontrar una puerta que llegue a algún lugar.

Recuerde: cuatro segundos para inhalar, cuatro segundos para sostener. Ahora:
exhale un domingo soleado de infancia.
Páramo de agua.
Ahora: vierta la consciencia en un charco de balneario.

Asomé el rostro y no encontré nada.
Recuerde: la memoria es tan ciega como un espejo.
 Me alejé y las chispas de sol brincaban.
Ahora: tambor líquido. Haga espuma con sus dedos arrugados. Juegue toda la
tarde durante diez minutos.

Advertencia: tiempo transcurrido. Usted se encuentra en el *Leteo*. Advertencia:
aquí la prisa es peligrosa pero la demora es la muerte.

Alarma: despertar, por favor, despertar.

Notificación: comprar aromatizantes sintéticos. Hoy es martes de frutas y
verduras en el supermercado.

Ya despierto,
cubro la ventana y recojo mis restos
de sol.
Otras vidas son los recuerdos.

Polvo

Rogelio de Jesús Cisneros

Escuchas los latidos
y sigues el origen en
voz baja
oyes tu nombre.

Caminas hacia adentro
te cubres
bajas la vista

tomas un plumero como bastón

te dispones a quitarle el polvo a tus recuerdos a
los retratos
a las horas
a las cosas.

Llegas al fondo del pasillo
sientes una puerta
enciendes la luz
y ves un espejo.

Lo que anhelas
ya fue en otro sitio
el camino está detrás de ti
pero ya no es camino
es memoria
es el tiempo
es aire

El tiempo
dejó una huella
y el aire la toca

el tiempo
borró tu imagen
y el aire dibuja otra.

Sol

Rogelio de Jesús Cisneros

Descubrí al sol escondido detrás de los árboles
lo esperé con los ojos casi cerrados
para fingir que no lo veía

sentí sus manos tibias haciéndome cosquillas en la cara

cuando abrí los ojos
todo estaba blanco,
no pude ver nada.

Ya sé porque se esconde detrás de los árboles.

Fear

Guy S Duke

The trip has been long
the stops infrequent,
and now I need to pee.

Far from anywhere
but full of people,
a rest stop like any other.

A public restroom,
taken for granted
my entire life,
until now.

I have never felt so noticed before in my life
and I am not comfortable at all.

The briefest of pauses
as he washes his hands.
A side-eyed glance at the air-dryer
and muttered disapproval
as I walk past to use the stall.

I stay for longer than needed.
Waiting.
Hoping he leaves and no one else comes in.

When I finally get up
the way is clear,
the room is empty.

But the fear of what may await me outside
inexorably creeps through my very being.

And nothing happens.
I get back in the car
and we're on our way once more.

But now I know the fear,
and it intimately knows me.

Dr. Jesus Presents: The All-Consuming Politician-Errr
Juan Manuel Pérez

They're eating our dogs
They're eating our cats
They're eating four-legged things like that

They're eating our birds
They're eating our turds
They're eating so many unhappy words

They are eating our "this"
They're eating our "that"
They're eating up all our "wackity-wack-wack"

They're eating our hats
They're eating our bats
They're even eating those democrats

They're eating our things
They're eating our thongs
They're eating up everything we know is wrong

But let's suppose one day that they finally stop eating
So that maybe then, they may stop competing
And then and maybe only then, and maybe no other time than then,
They may truly earn their political seating

Hibiscus Mahajad
Anthony Ripp

I know how this ends with her wearing Manolo Blahnik's to a discotheque.
Haven't you ever had to let the beat...........drop?
The city's going off and I'm a poet,
how hard could this be?

Enter Hibiscus Mahajad.
Back door, after hours, kids asleep,
back to work it out with me.

In her living room, there's an oil of a French nude in the ghetto,
Smoking cigarettes,
waking up the city.

Underneath the old neon sign that used to blink Jesus saves,
I danced with the devil.
Red shoes, black dress, porcelain faced,
and gorgeous.
Haven't you ever seen the Maltese falcon?
She was just like that.
Dramatic,
addicted to silk and fragrance.
I stirred my Brandy with a nail and read her poems

She was sick and I was Rumi eyed, nostalgic.
It was perfect,
we were made for this.
For fairy tales.

And who the fuck is Alice?!?!
A white rabbit comes in the night and tries to take me.
Sometimes it's a hatter, mad.
She's mad too, temptation
She was that
She was always that to me.

the Flora and Fauna of a Texas Suburb
Kim Denning

a mapled sort of leaf
curls under sun
hanging on air

exotic, vagabond
unseasonal in red saturation
caught in the fate of gravitational wind

set to a path of migrant tumbling
it cartwheels on delicate limbs
across the emerald varietals of broad,
sidewalk-less lawns

ticking, lifting strong
over pebbled asphalt
past drought-plagued rain gutters

drifting, past cut-out houses
their cookie colors popping,
bursting in realtor delight
framed by nurtured greens
fortified fairways, and wet-nursed yards

leaf rests.
detained
captured
by grassy blades
all manicured to perfection
by disembodied Brown hands
and myths of American Dream

Bruise
Arturo Cortez Jr.

- I remember, at the age of 4, asking Mom and Dad what lightning was made out of. They said, "It's probably made out of something able to guard the skies and its people. You can ask the angels one day. Now, go back to sleep for God's sake".

- I remember driving in Rio Bravo by what seemed to be an execution, cold blooded, by the cartel. As I turned to face forward, stepping on the gas, just a few blocks away, there was a *Conjunto,* day drinking, and performing *corridos* to themselves.

- I remember when they first built the Rio Bravo- Donna International Bridge and thinking, "This is it. All eyes will be on Rio Bravo now."

- I think God's favorite letter in the alphabet is the letter "Ñ/ñ".

- I remember every Monday morning in 90s Fahrenheit, singing the Mexican National and Tamaulipas anthems, as if they were pacts, solemn as our school uniforms.

- I remember being called *Negro, El Snicker, prieto, Memín Pinguín* while studying at a private school in Rio Bravo. I didn't know how to fight nor was never good with comebacks, so I stayed silent.

- I remember teaching English in *Mexico* to young adults. One time, there was an old lover in my class, and besides having to commit to the lesson, we both had the job to pretend not to know each other.

- All surgeries performed on me know Mexico only.

- I remember crossing to Rio Bravo, but immediately turning back to the US crossing line, since *balaceras* were taking place and we were not to disturb *them.*

- I remember looking up for answers in the forming of clouds, but the skies just showed me their bruises instead.

- I remember crossing to Mexico with Dad and my brother *Luis,* and right after the checkpoint, busting out the ice cold Bud Light six pack as we were on our way, hoping no *balacera* will turn us back.

Faith
Sidney King

I believe in Jesus
But I do not think he's real.
And God does not exist
But we still brokered a deal.
Our deal, it went like this:
I said, please show me a way
To find out how to live this life
Without wasting away.

And the God who did not exist
Did not answer my prayer
Cause he does not know how to live,
In this we make a pair.
But God said you should find a way
To let go and forgive.
You might find some peace in life
If you just had some grace to give.

God does not exist, I know
Because He speaks of grace
Like it's something that He gives
As more than a small taste.
And I know I'm not better,
And I hold grudges too.
But I guess you cannot be God
Unless you can follow through.

So God and I, we've reached some terms
On which we can agree:
It's up to him what's right and wrong,
But I'm the one who's free.

Lack of Steel

Braxsen Sindelar

Your steel bends to my growl.
The sword you wield, curving,
Bending, around my soul.
I'm not some cute cheetah.
I won't run from the blade.
In fact, I'll embrace it.
You'll be back anyway.
Maybe Monday at 5.
Or prowling through the night.
Waiting for my claw strike.
As the clock strikes midnight.
When you are dead tonight.
From unmerciful hands.

Battle of Tilottama
Suranjit Gain

Battle of Tilottama;
historical moment
Living Durga from house to house;
Asura's gang tortures.
Ran Chandi wake up!
Let the devil be afraid.
Leave hair colic!
The mistake of touching fire
They will no longer;
a woman's eyes will not be filled with tears.
Abandoning self-respect with;
Tilottama brought about women's awakening.
A new chapter has begun;
Come forward Miss World.
With great man;
The monster trembled with fear!

Eucalyptus Trail
After a painting by Gary Barten

Miriam Sagan

1. Interview With the Landscape

Where did you come from?
Where are you going?
That pungent medicinal smell
Takes me back
To when I was young, in love, and bitterly
Unhappy
Where none
Of my pairs of shoes
Were appropriate
For walking a trail.

2. What's On Your Plate?

Ink on paper
Asemic writing
In the twisting intersection
Of leaves and sunlight
Oil for the masters
And acrylic because
The last century
Was the one
We were born in.

3. Crows, Spheres, Boats, and Methods of Transportation

How fortunate that this world
Can still surprise us:
An aging—aged—body
On the path or on a trail.
Things that once

Stayed on the surface
Now reveal a crack—
The child I once was.

4. Interview With Your Hunger

How is your world
And everyone in it?
How are you?
Where are you located?
Painting with that amazing
Feat of evolution;
The opposable thumb.

5. What is Eucalyptus Good For?

To clear the mind
To soothe cough
To attract caterpillars, bees, pollination
To repel mosquitoes
And fear
To heal this wound.

6. Map of The Different Trails

Far view. Just a few steps more.
Watch out for snakes. Compassion.
Leading nowhere. Star-shaped flower.
Leading everywhere.

Brood XIX and the Ancestors (Magicicadas)

"for they still continue on Singing until they die"
—Benjamin Banneker, African American naturalist

Dr. Grisel Y. Acosta

the news calls them ugly
too loud, a nuisance, these insects
originally from Asia, Africa, the Americas
but I've always loved their melody

I walked along to it at Pleasant Valley
years ago, strolling along the side
oats grama grasses and swamp thistle
hot and sweaty, heading for the pool

this was the time when I raced
kids, quick laps in the chlorinated
water—I always won—and then
got sick from the chemicals, all while

the cicadas sang, wanting to attract
mates in their chorus trees, buzzing
no one complained of the sound—
this love slow jam track was a hit

everywhere all the time, natural
and we felt at home in this world
of goats and chickens, outside
the city of street ball and chain link

sometimes we were quiet, just listening
to the whirring drone, sometimes
we sang too, under Basswood or Red Oak

pop songs in English, classics in Spanish

we tried to ignore the moments we, too,
were called ugly on the news, a nuisance
recalled our time in nature, when different
voices came together in harmony

THE ARROWS PIERCING THE BOSOM ARE NOT ARROWS

Guna Moran

After great pain,
a formal feeling comes
                    - Emily Dickinson

Moving at an electric speed
The arrows get wedged on the bosom
Do not pierce through
Like a bullet

Only one bosom
Pricking-poking of so many arrows

In raw flesh
Sorrow of blue clotted blood
Furrows continuously

So tiny
This heart
How will it bear
The stinging of poison-arrows
Shot by you
The master archer

Musings on Artificial Intelligence
Michael Shoemaker

"AI is a fundamental risk to the existence of human civilization in a way that car accidents, airplane crashes, faulty drugs, or bad food were not."
—Elon Musk, Tesla & SpaceX chief executive
or another billionaire that likes technology

I read that AI is intended to be a "question and answer" advisement counselor or tool, but once all of us realize that AI fills even the rudimentary yet partial function of "thinking" what will prevent human nature's distaste for the hard work of thinking from kicking in and surrendering most decision-making over to a new lord? Yes, the human drive for autonomy, independence and freedom is strong, but is it greater than the domineering creature's comfort of ease? In a bet, unfortunately, I am not putting my ready money on independence and freedom to win this battle in most cases. Think of human history. How often have humans surrendered the thinking function not to sophisticated technology, but to drunken, petulant, childish, temperamental and imperfect authoritarian dictators or oligarchs? How will humankind avoid wholesale global rulership when there will be siren smooth songs telling us that this collective human thinking tool is wiser, smarter and healthier than our own thoughts and beliefs? I intend to use AI in harmony with my individual thoughts and thinking cap in place. Is this feasible? Even if it is feasible, is it probable? The call will be to use the Good and leave the Bad of AI. Can I ask how that worked out with the Internet? It's ok, you don't have to defend a person's right to be continuously focused on the Internet for eight hours daily. They have the right no matter how damaging it may be. You have the right to self-determination, but how long can you preserve that right under a barrage of conflicting messages that have different motivations and intentions? Admittedly, I do not know much about AI, but because I breathe and bleed like you, I think I can weigh in. What can or will you teach your children or grandchildren about this now? Will they listen or are they already plugged into the AI mainframe? What will be the arc in the next hundred years?

Buckle up and hold on. I think we are in for quite a bumpy ride.
Will humanity prevail? Probably, but in what form?
Will it be intelligent and caring?

Beauty, Beyond, and Define
Logan Dovalina

In our beautiful days
Beyond the opal hours of time
Are choices that define our lives
In the supple years of becoming
Endowed by our mothers and fathers
Is a seed so pure, so becoming
Ever becoming
Yet, in hazy days, scarred by the sears of time, we become calloused and
frayed Looking for what remains, if any, remains
Our mourned love, of beauty and time aching away
Comes a dark abyss to unforgiving years of will
Forcing our souls away
Yet we love
We feel the breadth of a warm embrace
Or the prick of a summer's love undecided
The infinity of our roots becoming
Ever becoming
Our souls' unarmed attempts, brazen, are treks to the stars in search of
completeness, a long-awaited completeness
In an odyssey of authenticity – falling to the depths of our
hearts We share the sunbeams of our lives, painting the
infinity
Our days - oh, our many days
Like liquid sun pouring a dappled sky
In our beauty, beyond, and define

FRAGMENTS OF ABSENCE

John Chinaka Onyeche

I am yet to know what it is
that a photograph holds for a boy
who misses his father when the union is over.
Today, in Guinea, New Papua,
a boy posed alone in a picture, waving his hand—
a way to say, I miss him whom I called Father.
This is over eight months of savaged contact,
and the cameraman knew nothing about this.
How in every lens and capturing of this moment,
the boy's pose speaks volumes
of loneliness and a world without meaning.
Yesterday, this picture was handed over to me.
I stared deep into his heart through his eyes,
to speak of the brokenness behind them—
how he held home and fatherhood
behind unspoken words that the mother
knows not but justifies the savaging
of the bridge more mundane than her son's
brokenness and aches that he lives with.
But in every pose for a picture, he speaks out:
Here, I am speaking for this emptiness—
this cloudy sky full of rain but unable to rain,
to wash out from my heart this vacuum
created when the parents choose to separate
without any sense of the aftermath for their kids.

a radio of ham
Jeannette Zallar

What is it you hear in those distortions?
What attracts you, the person I love, in that colorful waterfall?

You speak of harmonics and frequencies and channels and stations I hear static,
faint noises, and see colorful waves within a small window

You excitedly show me maps from NOAA, maps translated from a burst of
noise. I see something I could find just as easily online, or on my phone.

You tell me to get beyond my technicians license, to join you on the radio of
ham. I see something I literally did merely so I could understand you talk.

What is it that you hear, night after night, hunched over your desk? I see you,
leaning into your work, and you haven't eaten in like five hours. I counted.

What within a numbers station calls to you, a siren's lure from a person unknown?
What causes your introspection, the person I love, within codes and hidden meaning?

You must have linked me at least twenty images of what your radio can pick up.
I see your passion, your spirit, something which truly highlights your mind.

You tell me day after day of your digital adventures in science and mathematics.
I, the artist you say you love, fall a bit more behind with each advancement.

Maybe you're asking yourself what I see in my stories, in my poems. Why must
they always be writing, always be thinking so much, you might say.

That's why I sit in your room and listen to you listen to the radio, because I love
you. It's a part of who you are, and whatever makes you happy, it's part of you too.

Chicharrón de Emoción
Alejandra Sánchez Alanís

We are people of purpose walking in steps of intent
deliberate within every breath pisamos con fe
our existence a rosary decadent shamanic chants
holy and floral water grief and resurrection
we're preamble of miracles the sign
of the cross protects us padre hijo y
espíritu santo

somos dichos de las abuelas y mal ojo turco
semilla de venado y cristales sacred
archaeological sites cuidado donde
pisas y bondad de Xochiquétzal y
Coatlicue expansion of spirit and
screams of indigenous gall
we're feathered Mexica y Maya güeras
 igual que apiñonadas
somos rebelión indígena escucha el tambor
bleeding wound of colonization sangramos
descendientes de gitanos Romani y Arabe
our molecules combat another
somos nómadas dejando madres patrias
in our pockets centavos de caló tex-mex y castellano

somos descendientes de la sierra
Majalca somos norteños son
Jarocho marimba danzón y mambo
de Pérez Prado somos cante de
Camarón y pasión de Lola Flores
cajón bulería y saeta triste triste triste
we're poesía of Paz Tafolla Lara-Silva y García Lorca

I understand why I get tongue tied
and why my zeta fights against my accent
we're ancestral poción mestizaje
somos capirotada costumbre y temazcal rituales
cilantro epazote y chile picado finito para pozole

worn out molcajetes y abuelas
secret arroz con leche somos
marchantes ambulantes
vendiendo
chicharrón de emoción sprinkled with chile
graffiti en las calles and penitents in churches
we're San Antonio de Padua y Yerba Buena San Francisco

somos el 'oleeeee' en La Plaza México tapas y
cañas ferias en Madrid una cofradía cargando
nuestro trono durante Semana Santa oraciones
a la virgen de Guadalupe y Macarena 'ten
piedad ten piedad' somos una sola hermandad a
sanctuary for another
recuerda there's no borderland in body mind
spirit spirit spirit

Aguante, igual
Alejandra Sánchez Alanís

Venimos caminando atrás el paso del serpiente
descendentes somos águila y nopal igual
desde desiertos áridos pampas vaqueras Mesoamérica Tikal y Aztlán
descendientes somos de origen mítico indígena comunal igual
trasladando desde La Mancha Castilla y León y Alhambra
descendientes somos reyes católicos emperadores caciques sultanes igual
existimos en cada apellido silaba náhuatl tilde y acento

Nacimos para el aguante en contra de dictaduras y racismo
aguante para el sol siembra y huelga igual aguante de pasar hambre y sed
nacimos para el aguante cruzando ríos escalando coyoteando contrabando
aguante de no asimilar ante lo puritana y el rojo blanco y azul igual
nacimos para trotar kilómetros en huaraches montar en botas de charro
descalzos en selvas y montañas algunos con broche de oro otros en
pobreza igual nacimos con el aguante de callo seguir caminando aunque
nos duele hasta el alma y morimos de sed igual somos el aguante sin
obligación que aguantar

pisamos hasta nos oyen los bisabuelos en el cielo despertándolos
pies firmes tocando la tierra como el tambor Africano quien llegó a costas
hablamos con convicción que nos oyen hasta la Casa Blanca no hay vuelta
atrás como trataron nuestros abuelos por prietos y no hablar inglés
existimos con ganas para hermanos quien no llegaron a cruzar
y en nuestros nombres Alejandra Adriana Aurora Leticia Sylvia Magdalena
Rosa enunciamos *take up space* di la *ah* con ganas alguien hizo el viaje
para nosotros cocinamos enchiladas bravas y fideo que absuelva pecados
somos consume de cariño cantamos el canto clavada en el pecho junto a
trio y mariachi para cortar las venas

> recuerda el tipo de sangre que corre dentro de tu cuerpo
> recuerda el silencio es cómplice
> recuerda no hay diferencia entre primera o segunda generación

somos somos igual como huellas digitales del colonialismo
recuerda el mismo dios no es político

    recuerda el sonido de tu apellido dilo con la fuerza de tus ancestros
recuerda donde no abren las puertas a uno rechazan a todos
somos somos igual como el aire que oscila dentro del pulmón
recuerda como heredaste privilegio llegaste al momento correcto
recuerda eres compasión mexicano bravura español resiliencia indígena
fuerza indominable africano criollo mestizaje poción de inmigración
recuerda sembrar un campo de maíz cempasúchil y alcatraz dentro
de tu corazón somos somos iguales como el amor revolucionario que
corre por nuestras venas somos cómo vestimos en el odio rechazo
aceptación o en humildad
= iguales

On St Mathias's Day
Bernard Pearson

After Judas had
Gone in to the shade
 Of the blood moon
While the sky was still quiet
And the earth slumbered,
Another stepped into the void,
Not really knowing if he was
A phoenix in a brush fire,
Or a blasphemer in
A god strewn world.

Anticipatory Grief

Danielle Harvey

My world has become smaller
Exhausted, I can do the bare minimum
I'm not elated
I'm mushy.
I feel nothingness, how could I go last week crying almost everyday to a stone today?
What's happening to me?
I got on this ride and I'm letting it take me to my next level
I'll miss the mezcal in Texas
The heart of this country, the middle.
I'm misunderstood right now
Who will get my anticipatory grief? Like I'm crazy, some of my friends think.
Like I could make up my response to what's happening?
I shouldn't be responding this way, but I am.
My mom is here, but I process her as if she is not.
My orbit is not the same, I'm sorry.
My loving mom is struggling and I'm supposed to carry on as if nothing is happening?
I can't, not possible, dead end.
I wish things were carefree like they were last February, before she got sick.
I keep waking up in Texas, in the middle, in a purgatory state, disassociated,
living as if she is gone but again, she is here.
I can do this, I can plunge forward.
My psychic said to make sure I have boundaries, to not lose my voice. I'll always
try to maintain and get better. Guide me, higher being, send me signals in my
body, and signs from opportunities. I trust myself.
When the cliffs are falling I'll reach out to grab myself and pull me in, landing
on a stable rock.

Fearless

Felicia Lopez

Walking into the great unknown
Looking for a new sense of purpose.
What drives me is my story—
Shaped from numerous stories,
Passed down from generation to generation.
I can walk away with pride
And my head held up high
Because I am—
Fearless.

Forced Perspective
Mayurakshi Chaturvedi

The portrait of Mr. Andrews and his wife hung over their home.
The ideal couple enjoying their respectful pastoral life.
He looked untouched and handsome in his arrogance.
His legs crossed at the ankle, the gun in his hand cocked towards the Gods.
His lovely wife looked innocent and harmless.
In her blue pinafore and silk slippers,
which were proper shoes for ladies,
and not meant for walking outdoors.
They sat on a beautiful bench under a tree,
at the very corner of their portrait, across from a winding road
that got lost in the fields.

The temperate Sun shone on them.
Brightly, but not too hot.
They looked on to their beautiful fields,
allowing the painter to focus greatly on the landscape.

They did not bother to venture out into the field.
That would spoil the fun of sitting at a distance
and enjoying a beautiful day.
The shocking reality was that enjoyment did not lie
in walking in the dirt, or tending to the crops, or cattle.
It rested in their minds.
And their declarations of the love they felt for nature.

Golden Length of Summer
Myra Tejada Rasmussen

During the golden length of summer, the kitchen curtains shine several shades of blue and this makes my mother fake-happy. She looks out the window for my father, fries eggs with extra butter. Wildberry preserves on the side. *Why is it called preserves?* I ask. *Because sugar keeps you sweet. Preserves your heart.* Then she kisses my forehead. The stench of burnt bacon from the blackened pan sizzles.

During the golden length of summer, my father toils the back-yard earth. In search of black soil. *Like tar* he says. *Needs to burn black as tar.* He stabs the hoe into the ground, small worms squirm to the top, suffocate in the air. I pick one up, watch it jiggle. Once, I saw my mother tear a worm in half. Both halves kept wiggling between her fingers, one more than the other. *Can it feel pain?* I asked. *No,* she said, as she dropped the pieces into her apron pocket. *Wouldn't it be nice to be a worm for a day? Bury yourself within quiet spaces of carrots? Swim in endless pools of heirloom tomatoes?*

During the golden length of summer, my mother learns to play with fire. The kind of fire that can leave skin scalloped. *I want to be cooked by love,* she says, then a match in her fingers and her world ablaze. *Does it hurt?* I ask her later while she lays on their bed covered in wet rose petals. *No,* she says as flakes of skin fall to the ground. Ants carry them away like sugar, back to the soil for my father to find.

Trust -*A dialogue between a mom and her high school son in the United States*
Megha Sood

There have been at least 58 school shootings in the United States so far this year, as of October 15. Fourteen were on college campuses, and 44 were on K-12 school grounds. The incidents left 28 people dead and at least 72 other victims injured - CNN's analysis of events reported by the Gun Violence Archive, Education Week and Everytown for Gun Safety.

You said, there is always a silver lining at the end of a dark cloud.
Golden pot of treasures and dreams at the end of a shiny rainbow.
Hidden musk in the pit of a deer, fairies dancing in the midst
of the starlit night, with raging emotions and endless delight.

Unicorns traveling deep ends of the forest werewolf serenading the moon,
with all its seeded fears. You said, there is always hope
You said this will be the last one and I will lose no one to this blinding fear.

The blue drills and screeching noises that startled me at night.
I shut my ears, tears falling, and dig myself in the softness of my pillow
only to be woken up by another nightmare from the deep ends
of this senseless fright.

There are countless deaths , names and dreams getting crushed in the bud.
The incessant, heartless killing blood lacing the corridors of my school.

You said the last time —there will be no more. No more dreams will get lost
in the dark. You said the violence will be less.
We have the voice, We have the power.

But we stay mute and numb till another news hit the headline
for this nation that loses its kids like damn flies.

And waits for another school shooting to report
amid the wails of countless mothers, inconsolable fathers,
mourning sisters and brothers to hold.

Grief laden with blatant lies screaming loud evermore.
You said the last time, there will be no more.
Now, there is no pain left for my soft body to endure.
This turnstile for grief should stop moving one day for sure.

I trusted you every time and it seemed fine.
I don't trust you anymore.

ONLY THEN AND NOT

Edward Lee

Your body turns to me,
as the flower might to water,
as the flower needs water,
if flowers do such a thing,
turning away
when the need for water
is met, if it must be met,

returning only
when water
is needed
again,

only then,
if that is what flowers do
when they need water,
as your body does
when it wants my touch,
but then again, perhaps
any touch will do.

I'm Trying to Write a Taco Poem. It's Not Going Very Well.
For Eddie Vega, San Antonio's Poet Laureate (2024-2027)
Violeta Garza

Those of us in San Antonio know what kind of life is worth living.
It always involves a filling of your choice inside a tortilla, if you're doing it right.

I wanted to add something spicy to the cannon of taco poetry,
but we already have a Taco Poet. And no one does tacos as good as Eddie. I don't
know if Dude actually makes good tacos.
I just know Dude writes about them so deliciously, se me caen las babas.

My attempt at writing a taco poem feels flimsy,
like the paper napkins from your favorite taquería–
the kind that are rectangular, thin and a little bumpy,
the kind that tear into shreds the moment you dab your mouth even a little
bit, so you have to grab three or four at a time,to sop up the mouth grease. My
attempt at writing a taco poem feels soggy,
like a to-go paper bag soaked with chorizo oil, pooled into the shape of La
Virgen de Guadalupe, because, of course it is, She is everywhere, here to bless us
all, even in our takeaway orders.
My attempt at writing a taco poem feels un poquito huango,
like the breakfast taco still wrapped in foil, but before even unfolding it to look
inside,you know it's your bean and cheese one, cos you poked it,
and it bends to your touch more than your papa con huevo. A huevo.

Taquitos de esos, de los buenos, the kind where you show up,
and the line is longer than you expected, out to the street,
and you almost drive away, but you stay,
cos those are the ones you've been memorizing on your tongue all day long.
They gonn' be worth the wait.

That sentiment? That vibe? It just might be warm enough to fill us all.

Amor de Cuatro Esquinas, Con Espinas y Azúcar
Violeta Garza

Tu amor duró solo un día. Tu calor, mucho menos.

Todavía te siento, corazón,
          después de estos mil años que han pasado
en solo unos cuantos meses.

Pero estoy convencida
de que mi lealtad a mi misma
es el trabajo
más audaz. Otro camino, otra luz propia.

De repente, al caminar, encuentro a una ave solitaria.
Ella quiere que alguien, no importe quien,
oiga su cantar.

Nosotras dos, nos encontramos solitas
          acompañadas de la esperanza.

Al siguiente momento, me da
mucho sentimiento y le canto a ella,
"Siéntate conmigo, pajarita,
con confianza."

Después de un cafecito,
las dos nos sentimos en familia.

Agárrense, todos, porque ahí les vamos,
y se van
a acordar
de nosotras.

Bluebonnets in Spring
Adrian Ernesto Cepeda

While we were hablando
on our weekly phone call,
from LA, Papi en San Antonio,
en la mitad of our conversación,
my father's voice drifted
in tones of a tristeza, memorias
he rarely shares happens every
few meses when he brings up
Mami. He starts off in static,
sounding distant in a tinge
of sadness with colors of remembering,
he shared *Manejando, I saw
Bluebonnets, today.* Papi had not
mentioned Bluebonnets in years
since Mami had passed. They would
always drive from la ciudad, seeking
her favorite flowers, as he was telling
me, because of the rain, they were
blossoming everywhere. Resounding
a momentary smile, hearing his sonrisa,
picturing a landscape of purple, telling me
about bouquet of fragrances, I imagine
Mami bringing a glass vase in car,
watching her gathering a handful
of flores to display en la mesa. Holding
back a drizzle of lágrimas, oyendo Papi
pausing his memory, clearing his garganta,
I was sensing a deeper conversation
beginning to bloom.

I Do
Rev. Tiffany "Queen T"

Neither the beginning nor the end
Shall bring our love to its end
Our love like a raging sea
The feeling, it really takes over me
I know we disagree and argue at times
And maybe we think, this will be our last fight
But know that the fight will never be over
Because for your love, I'd die like a soldier
I'd climb over mountains and run out through forests
If only to keep the love we have growing
God brought you to me in a time of grief
Little did I know that even after, you'd stay loving me
The final "I Do" with a FOREVER to go
I'll ALWAYS love you
From now until death
I DO…

Su bendicion
Cynthia Hernandez

Madrecita! Écheme su bendición, le dijo

Sabia que seria la ultima vez que la vería

Ya tenía alistado su morralito pal camino

Un pantalón dos camisetas tres truzas

Dos pares de calcetines un par de tenis

Y su chamarra preferida

La que su viejita que con tanto sacrificio le regalo pa navidad La foto de un Santito

Y la de su madre

Ella solo sabía que él saldría

Porque por fin encontró chance de trabajar

El pensó que la llamaría llegando con la buena noticia Mamita me cruce la línea de mojado

Pero no se modifique que ya llegamos

Usted solo pidele a Diosito que me vaya bien

Y no esté triste!

Que nada más guardo una lanita y me los traigo Pero él nunca tuvo la oportunidad

El coyote y la troca que llevaban se estrellara contra un semi Y ahí moriría

Ahí morirían sus sueños sus esperanzas

Un futuro entero

El logro llegar a la tierra de leche y miel

Sólo para encontrarse con la muerte

Ella se quedaría rezando a un Dios

Que no escucha a los pobres

Y esperando una llamada que jamás le llegaría Aquel día murieron dos

El luchando por una mejor vida

Y ella porque su partida le destrozaria el corazón

Si te encuentras lejos de tu tierra
Cynthia Hernandez

Si te encuentras lejos de tu tierra Y lejos de tu gente
Guardame en la mente
Y en el corazon

Porque yo te llevo
Hoy y siempre
Conmigo
Muy adentro
Como un gran tesoro
Como una bella canción

Y cuando al fin
Estemos juntos
Lado a lado
Frente a frente

Tomare tu mano y te recordare
Lo feliz que estoy de verte
Abrazarte y estar presente
Y lo agradecido que me siento
Porque Dios nos a regalado este momento Para llenar el
alma
De gozo y amor
Pa seguir dandole puro pa'delante

Que El te cuide y te guarde
Hasta que de nuevo estemos juntos los dos

Waiting to Die
Cynthia Hernandez

Waiting to die
As the calendar and the clock
Run out of
Days
Hours
Minutes
Seconds

T
  I
    M
      E

Standing still
Cynically laughing faces like ghosts
Come and go
Wanting your soul
One more moment
One more memory
Forgiveness
More love
Stoically welcoming the inevitable
It is that essence that you leave as the quiet guide for navigating The unknown
The impossible
That even in the unknowing, there is peace to be found I am not
ready to exist
In a world that you are not in
I will treasure you in my heart
Until my very own last dying breath

Oprah in Texas
R. Joseph Rodríguez

1998, Amarillo

Oprah sits in court
to be freed in speech.
Cattlemen want her quiet,
as she beefs with them.

Oprah unsettles beef
sales of the cattlemen
who want profits, wins.
The cattle remain silent.

Oprah lassos the theater stage
when she enters and waves.
The crowd claps and roars
and the eye of Texas, white.

Oprah wears yellows and
blues and reds with boots,
a power mic in hand.
A reckoning of sorts unfolds.

Oprah dons a cowgirl hat
and learns the two-step
dance with Patrick Swayze;
the world watches in glee.

The jury listens to libel laws.
And Oprah's name is cleared.
Yes, beef is for wholesale,
but not all want beef.

Oprah wonders words
to share about all this,
then says, "Free speech
not only lives, it rocks!"

Oprah's voice still rings
in towns that rise up
to be freed in speech
and deed for victory.

Juvenile
Kevin Adam Flores

I am not a poet who can dish out poems every day,
One after another, like some poetic prophet or pretender.

I'm a patient poet who, like a painter, looks at a blank canvas
And starts constructing life, slowly but surely, stroke after stroke,
Discovering a new color in the artwork for days, months, years.

I stare into a patterned tile wall, only fixated on the cracks between.
Somehow, they provide me peace because each crevice formed over time,
Like our imperfections from childbirth and a misinterpreted childhood.
From horny teenagers to settled down adults, past relationships and current hermits,
I don't know if they trek alone now, but I am missing the comforting company.
Adolescent love vanishes, perishes as my brothers,
The unlovable born to lie, cry, expire—like I—
Push me toward the edge, sending me off the deep end.

I cannot keep up with the clock hands, and nobody likes what they are doing.
I am a bedroom visionary, another suicide lover of poetry;
A sad man's pain mirrors his arduous art.

Perhaps I feel older than my alleged appearance since I'm killing my spirit faster;
My youth is bleeding out nostalgic memories, all at once through unclothed wounds.

Wishful thinking to be juvenile again—
However, I grant myself eternally young.

I do not hover but dangle:
Disengaged, dejected, dying,
Like witnessing an object being lost forever
In some meaningless background
Or like superheroes and magicians,
Their fake performance of grand illusion.

If my loved ones stood as a quiet audience
To observe my dramatic final act,
I wonder who would stand by
And watch me succeed,
Who would actually stop the show
And just catch me.

this love still beats in me
Linda M. Crate

you fell through my window
in slants of warm, pink sunset
that warmed my bones;

you shimmer across my memories
when i hear certain songs or watch
certain movies or when i see models
with features similar to yours or see
girls with pink hair or see pink cars
drive past me, i am reminded of you when
i see anything lord of the rings or hobbit
related, anything with faeries or vampires,
white roses—

rosefinch, i know i was wrong for
hurting you and i will forever live with
that regret;

but i cannot bury the love i have for you
for it still beats through my chest—

you were the most beautiful sun i have
ever come to known,
and i was hoping we could have that
fairy tale love and happily ever after which
happens in story books;

instead we have all these oceans between us.

Deber, Querer y Tener

Lisha Adela García

Tengo sed.
Tengo hambre de piel.
Break the chain
break the curse
      of past possession
          dile adios.

Part with gravity.
          Deja que las pisadas
          huecas de la memoria
          se vayan con la lluvia de merced.

Fill the breast cups
you so generously gave away.

    Muerde el miedo,   let it go!

       Amor Fati   ven a mi.

          Benvenuti lavender fingerprints on skin.
            Drum sacral sounds,
            drum deer
            drum sahuaro and ocotillo.

Suelta el susto
       breathe
       float on salty seas
       and plentiful starfish.

       Amor Fati   ven a mi.

Sanamé
veemé desnuda
oculta el camino de vigilia constante.

Imagine me whole   without black holes of swallow   a thirsty star.

Desviste la luna   ponme la cadena sin voz

      la que no conoce   el deber
      la que no se acuerda del   adiós.

Things no one Knows About Border Me

After Lana Hechtman Ayers

Lisha Adela García

> *Ahora es un poco de ceniza y de gloria*
> —*Jorge Luis Borges*

There is a river flowing down my middle with a whirlpool in my chest. Its foam devours and surges leaving droplets of my passing on a desert floor.

I learned to parent myself by looking in the mirror after my brother left me for a fungus in his lung.

I am the woman who gave the wizard his words: *pay no attention to the man behind the curtain.*

I can wild-flower myself to different grasses and winter as a purple viola in full bloom.

I have prayed on Hopi land, bowed my head to the eagles of First Mesa and the ravens of the Petrified Forest.

Ancestors hold me hostage around the rib cage, parse healing by the teaspoon.

I have learned to shelter in the places birds hide during a storm.

Justice is my favorite card in the Tarot although I still lack evidence from the Moon.

I don't have confidence in love, it appears too quickly and makes my eyes water. It is a disproportionate surrender, flirtation, sinking with no return guarantee.

The pilgrims inside break the bones of normalcy and bully me to write.

I wrote a pain depreciation schedule so I could breathe free before I die.

I have Herculean skin with many stitches and shock resistance ... a Comedia Divina for the parts of my body I excused for being traumatized.

I need God to be a simple unheralded invitation of feminine wisdom.

The mockingbirds inside me are a sign of dismantling, I am skilled now at calling them home.

The cardinals inside me are a sign of mourning, I am skilled now at building them nests.

I like you to hold my hand, especially if you are wearing blue and sitting beside me.

On the Street

Doug Croft

I want to write of vagabonds, miscreants, and wanderers.
Poems of troubled souls.
But I have never lived on the street.

I want to write of lost individuals
surviving in concrete campgrounds.
Sharing leftover food scraps.
Yet I have never lived on the street.

I want to write from perspectives of newspaper blankets,
oversized clothes and cardboard shoes.
Unkempt hair and hunger.
Hunger for anything.
Hunger for everything.
However, I have never lived on the street.

I write instead of what I know.
Nature, love, and broken hearts.
I write about social injustice and the human condition.

I sometimes write music and light.
People I know and American collective.
I write of elderly, Christianity, and simple little verses.

I met a lady serving her Lord.
Ministering to those lost to society,
displaced from work, living conditions, or family connection.
Consumed by ravages of addiction or mental disorders.
Vulnerable to the elements of exposure.

She shared her spellbinding poem.
Depths of brokenness, vagrancies, and struggle.
So moved I whispered, "I wish I could write poems like that."
Her thoughtfully warm and soft reply, "Ah, but you cannot,
for you have never had to live on the street."

What I Do In the Garden
Michael Owens

While clipping rose blooms mid-summer
I walk the empty garden path and pull up
memories from my days on this earth.

Tornado rips away our paid-for home
the day after we had moved for a new job
creating a windfall of cash for our new home.

Car stops suddenly on a crowded road
as a barrier slams down in front of me
before a train speeds past saving my life.

A cluster of lightning bugs draws me to the
edge of a balcony moments before a long
a branch crashed where I was standing.

Despondent sitting with my aging mother
my daughter calls to tell me the test is
positive I will be a grandmother.

Anxious sitting in an empty waiting room
at the hospital when the doctor steps
through the door and flashes thumbs up.

My Church asks for Spanish speakers to volunteer
as translator guides for families seeking
their children detained by U. S. Customs Service

These are the thoughts that fill my mind
when I am in the garden.

Emergence: A Dragonfly's Path
RescuePoetix

Like the myth that dragonflies live for a day,
months and years go by to complete cycles
unseen

Leaving one life behind for another,
discovering what fits with newly bejeweled wings,
layers deep, flying backwards,

away from what no longer serves

Molting is a natural process, making way for new growth,
time and again reinvention adds to myth
that I am a I was once

Catching moments along the way,
slowing to understand that
what sticks isn't always to remain

Fluttering about, not always with clear vision
When things pass,
they are past and remain there;

moving in six directions lends to doubt falling away

So fleeting, the time
of maturity and wisdom …

Most of my life spent learning,
rediscovering, reimagining
that the now is more precious that what was

I've learned to be comfortable in all surroundings:
On water, on earth, within me, not ready to land yet,

still discovering what that means;
prosperity, harmony, happiness
all the while eating the wind

while weighing
the worth
of my soul

Future Revolution

Carl Scharwath

"We believe that the supreme task of art in this day and age is consciously to take an active part in preparing the revolution."

—Andre Breton

Silent electric whispers
Ignite-
Spark-
not in the streets, but in the heartbeats of those unseen,
whose nightmares were the chains of the old world.

A revolution not with guns
Words-
Dance-
like binary fireflies, illuminating the night
of forgotten promises

We rise, not as soldiers
Shadows-
Unchained-
voices a symphony in the digital world,
forging new bonds of understanding.

In the cities of tomorrow
Freedom-
Song-
our hopes painted on the crumbled walls of virtual stone,
each stroke is a testament to our collective aspirations.

We stand as conquerors
Heartbeats-
Promise-
over the horizon of possibility; each link a story, a life,
each breath the sweet air of a new revolution.

Caramelo

Connie Ramírez

Sandia sazonada–
A sweet chupetin,
A reminder of Mexican summers In a lollipop,
Sweet & spicy chupetin.
Picante tamarindo–
Candy from a tree,
A memory of Nana's casa
Eating mango pulparindos,
Mis primos y yo en el jardín.
Leche quemada–
Mexican cajeta "honey",
And some memories of Celaya, Aldama candy wafers,
A creamy candy dream.
Its wrapper has a red rose–
Powdered peanuts, so crumbly. Mi
amiga gifted me a whole box,
Marzipan is a luscious, lovely
dream– A mixture of caramels and
golden honey.

Black Christmas Nigeria
Joseph C Ogbonna

This Christmas I sang a carol like a dirge.
I heard the news about deaths caused by stampedes.
From north, east and west, tales of woes did emerge,
Of famished multitudes trodden under foot.

Pregnant women and boisterous youths, each mowed down,
As their empty stomachs yearned loudly for their fill.
Misery and tears have deluged each Nigerian town;
Ibadan, Okija, and peaceful Abuja.

A philanthropist's gesture became their nightmare,
When Christmas charity became Christmas hell.
When the desire to improve human welfare
Led scores of indigents to untimely exits.

Era un hombre
Ramiro Hernández Restrepo

agobiado de primavera
con alas de amor encogidas
dando puños en silencio
a una mujer de bruma
y un niño cogido de sus manos.
En vez de sueños
realiza sombras
y siluetas que se deshacen
tras los muros.

Un poema
Ramiro Hernández Restrepo

si no es pedrada en la cien
es un tamal yerto
de palabras de honda.

Gloria del martillo que hizo fuego
Alejandro Zapata Espinosa

pecando en las rosas tendidas.
El mármol fue abortado
y entonó partos de luna.
Lirios que supieron callar
los cisnes insomnes
y las esferas sin dueño.
Cardos que rebasan la espera
encienden el limbo reflejo
copia de lontananza.
Enciérrate
huye de los caprichos
que te han robado la entraña
antes de que pases
a adornar el lecho cómplice.

Dóblase el cayado:
Alejandro Zapata Espinosa

la oveja inservible
su espuma regocija los cortafuegos
y da señales
a la marcha descalza.
Una visión pudo detener
los trozos que componen el sombrero
y pactaron dejar a medias la oración
que resucitaba con brizna
el hidalgo en dos partes mocho.

A Yahaira

Alejandro Zapata Espinosa

Cola de diablo fuiste
mimo de bruja e himno al infame;
abriste el recodo para una miga
de los santos negados
y diste a lamer la pulpa
que no se da en el cielo.

Soliloquy in a Graveyard
Anne Estevis

I stood on your grave today
looking down at the earth that imprisons you.
There aren't many things
 I wouldn't give to have you back again
for a day or an hour -- even minutes.
Then I could tell you all the things
I should have said -- but didn't.

I stood on your grave today--
lonely, angry, afraid -- because I miss you,
your silly sense of humor,
your smile, and the love we shared.
I'm angry because death took you from me
and changed my world forever.
I'm afraid of life without you.

I stood on your grave today
wondering if there is a loving god
and a heaven where good souls go.
It's hard to believe in life after death and
that we'll ever meet again. But who knows?
The fate that brought us together
may do the same again.

Poetry of solitude

Steve Anc

Oh, souls in solitude!
There is a consolation in defeat.
There is caution in victory.
Joy and suffering are twin dancers of life
They dance together long into the night.

Yes!
 Life is a tale of lessons-
Sometimes so sane and sweet;
With a blessing and a curse
But when a man is tired of living
He is tired of life.

Don't stare too long in space,
And do not hide from life-
Though it is bad, maybe worse;
But it has lines of sunny shine
That makes the blessing of a curse,
With optimism hard to beat.

Some days are bright.
Some days are boring.
Misfortune is a bitter pill,
But there is faith in the sky-
A benediction in disguise;
Because there is comfort in the worst of woe.

In Time And Times Be
Katrenia Grace Busch

If my tongue could speak,
I'll tell you what it would say—
In time and times, it would seek
After your words night and day

If my ears could listen,
I'll tell you what they would hear—
In time and times beckon
To ensure your voice was clear

If my hands could work,
I'll tell you what they would do—
In time and times smirk
At the thought of seeing you

If my eyes could see,
I'll tell you what a sight—
In time and times be
Of both day and night

If my heart could feel,
I'll tell you what it would say
In time and times steal
It's speech from what I pray

Today, Gaza needs you more
Abdulrozaq Tasleem Fholarin

Come all!
Let me tell you how it started:
a body of flame was once seen
floating in the sky. Like radio-active peppers.
Someone thought it was a shooting star.
Someone thought it was a big fire fly.
It happened. When the boys were playing
In the street. Girls. Drawing henna on themselves.
It happened. It happened. It happened.
Where do I find the word for this ruin?
Today, a house becomes glass. Grinded to debris.
Its bricks become a food chain to the black soils.
Today. A building. A boy. Thousand of wails.
Well-placed holes on roads. The sun is hot too.
Today, lord, Gaza. Gaza needs you.
More than water.   More than food.
The news feed is   lord—you, are what
awful like bile.   Gaza craves for.
                 God;
                 Gaza...

A raven
Alexander Limarev

A raven soars over the cliff,
Like a restless soul
Seeking its eternal refuge.

AN ODE TO ADOLESCENCE
John Grey

Adolescence
is like a library of books
all open at different pages,
daring you to read them all at once.

It's the moon shining down
on the clasp of your diary,
and heights marked
with pencils on a wall.

It's the clear blue air
of short-sleeved summers.
Or bedroom winters
with the invisible guitar
and the first awkward steps
of your forever dance.

It's head bowed,
scribbling a love poem
in a notepad,
celebrating,
with clumsy phrases,
the opposite sex
while still wondering…
opposite of what?

Spring Splits in Two

A Hua with translation by Xuelan Su and Ziying Fan

Spring Breeze Road hasn't seen the spring.
The swallows haven't returned to Swallowtail Park.

In Pear Tree Village*, the mist that fills my eyes
Is a spring surging from deep in my heart.

"Some dear ones have gone away, and still some words
Pierce the heart like 10,000 arrows."

Spring splits in two. Delight ascends.
Sadness fades away.

Someone cradles a candle in both hands, but waits 'til nightfall to near the shore.
Chilling winds return home again.

— In the distance, grass and trees lament.
Gray magpies fly.

Among the annuals

Only the small white flowers bloom. Only the lonely
Can know why they persist.

Only someone on the verge of crying can understand
What's kindled amid the blooming and withering.

Blanketing the mountains and grasslands, a brief but magnificent display.
Blanketing the mountains and grasslands, one's sorrow
The sorrow of many.

*Pear Tree Village is an imagined, spiritual home, a comfortable place that can
contain one's grief, a sunny and safe place for the soul, a place where all manner
of ideas and emotions have the space to be.

春分

A Hua with translation by Xuelan Su and Ziying Fan

春风路没有见过春风
燕尾洲也没飞过燕子

在梨树镇，我眼眶里的潮润
是心底向上奔涌的泉水

"有些人已经走远，有些话
仍是万箭穿心"

春天一分两半，欢喜升腾
悲伤下行

有人手捧烛火，等夜色靠岸
再送清风回家

——远处，草木骊歌四起
灰喜鹊在飞

途中的一年蓬

只开小白花，只有孤独的人
才懂得它的执着

只有一个想哭的人，才明白
它的开开落落里，点燃了什么

漫山遍野里，一年蓬开得盛大
漫山遍野里，一个人的悲伤
也是很多人的悲伤

Soy De...
Yari "Porta Rock"

Soy de la isla del encanto
100por35
Tierra de grandes poetas, escritores, cantantes,
boxeadores, peloteros, jueces de courte supremo, actores y guerreros

Soy de donde El Magnífico "The Great One"
Roberto Clemente nació y la salsa
tan sabroso y caliente cojio su sabor
y donde la bomba y plena suena su tambor

Soy de dónde Bad Bunny se lo comió
con su apagón y el reggaeton puso al mundo
a perriar con su sazón

Soy de donde el Mar
toca el sol y las olas te cantan una canción
mientras las brisas te refrescan del calor

Soy de donde Agueybana el valiente
Betances, Albizu, Lolita y Cancel pelearon por la patria y libertad
de nuestra gente !

Soy de donde Se le pide la bendición a sus
seres queridos y se dice buen provecho cuando ven a una persona comiendo

Soy de donde el grito de
CAPICU ! indica que alguien
Gano en un juego de domino

Soy de donde
Celebramos las navidades con
Parrandas y recibimos los 3 reyes magos después del año nuevo

Soy de la mezcla de razas taino, africano
Y español soy de donde viene el ron caña, y la décima de la montaña
Soy de donde la estrella brilla en la bandera
SOY DE PUERTO RICO PARA QUE LO SEPAN

Las plegarias
Diosa Xochiquetzalcóatl

Santa María, Madre de Dios,
no pido oro, ni pido plata
pido que me ahuyentes del malviviente
y toda aquella gente ingrata.

Reina de todos los santos,
Morenita milagrosa,
permíteme verlo divorciado
para por fin convertirme en su esposa.

Matriarca de los mexicanos
jamás me desampares.
Que todas mis citas de hoy en adelante
sean espectaculares.

Madre de la misericordia,
Tú que eres tan grande
no dejes que viva mi suegra conmigo
ni aunque Dios nos lo mande.

Lupita de mi corazón,
Refugio de los que sufren
aleja a mi hermano de mis pretendientes,
no vaya ser que se asusten.

María del santísimo rosario,
Esposa de San José
líbrame de todos los tóxicos
como el último desgraciado que se fue

Nuestra Señora de Guadalupe,
Reina de las Américas
ayúdame a juntar unos centavitos
para hacerme la cirugía cosmética

Virgencita del Tepeyac,
Diosa de la raza de bronce
concédeme bajar unas libritas de más
ya de perdis unas once.

Virgen de las vírgenes,
Casta y Clemente
haz entender a papá
que no me caso con Don Vicente.

Camino de los ángeles,
Consuelo de los migrantes
te pido que me protejas
y que no me retachen como antes

Auxilio de los cristianos,
Causa de nuestra alegría
no me dejes caer en el vicio
de llegar a la panadería
ni recordar a ese bueno para nada
ni de noche ni de día
elimina de mi las tentaciones
de comer taquitos con mantequilla
y también te ruego y te suplico,
ante tu altar y de rodilla,
que nunca se me olvide que soy mujer completa
y que no vengo de ninguna costilla.

O, María, Madre mía, Fuente de la verdad
ya no permitas el patriarcado, la misoginia ni las jerarquías
haz que recuerden todititas las niñas que son unas Diosas divinas

O, María, Madre mía, fuente de la verdad
¡Así sea!
¡Así sea!
¡Así sea!

Imperceptible
Diosa Xochiquetzalcóatl

Entre mis muslos se desborda un río incontenible,
sin embargo, nadie lo ve.
¿Será que mi angustia es invisible?

Dentro sonrisas de mármol infalible,
se escuchan los quejidos de Perséfone (mientras que)
entre mis muslos se desborda un río incontenible.

Escritas están en la enciclopedia de mi útero ilegible
los traumas que nunca, a nadie le conté.
¿Será que mi angustia es invisible?

Existe en mi matriz una herida irreversible
herida ancestral de la Malinche y su bebé (mientras que)
entre mis muslos se desborda un río incontenible.

De mi vientre escurre un llanto violento y temible,
río volcánico y tumultuoso de la Diosa Pelé.
¿Será que mi angustia es invisible?

Por más que le pregunto al Dios insensible
simplemente, no entiendo el porqué.
Entre mis muslos se desborda un río incontenible.
¿Será que mi angustia es invisible?

El tlatoani
Diosa Xochiquetzalcóatl

I.
Tizoc
el que hace penitencia
el olvidado

II.
Tizoc
la que se juntó con mi tatarabuelo
la que tuvo hijos
olvidados

III.
Tizoc
la que se creó con mi bisabuela
la que se casó con un hijo de la chingada
la golpeada, violentada, maltratada
la que se quedó sin sus hijos
la olvidada

IV.
Tizoc
el que emigró a los Estados Unidos
el que tiene hijos regados
quienes, tal como lo dicta el legado,
han quedado
en el olvido

V.
Tizoc vive
lejos de su lengua
lejos de su gente
lejos de su tierra

el tlatoani
sigue retoñando
con todo y penitencia

Tizoc vive
lejos de su lengua
lejos de su gente
lejos de su tierra

Dec. 31st, 1997

Immanuel A. Garcia

I was delivered without hesitation
in a room that my mother made hers
with cesarean signatures.

I hear about it on holidays
and trips to the beach.

My mother relays how her organs
became mine in an instant.
How the invention of silence
got stuck between her wisdom teeth.

Cloaked adults
provided sterilized applause
as my mother noticed the shift in room
temperature through the love-sized hole in her
torso.

It was as if an elephant sat down on my
chest and began to do a circus trick.

She says smiling at me
like I'm the murderer she helped get away with it.

An oil spill of light
the crescendo of holy smoke personified.
gunpowder in the air
and a Bible ajar
from where my name rustled out of the pages
like a cage to a mutt still learning what having a home means.

I still move in that room
under a sky-blue blanket that asks questions in a
tongue most often confused with fireworks.

In other words
I was born on the breath of a farewell.
Reciting the memories of an elephant
who recalls the melody as something too fragile to part with.

Anger is Sometimes a Form of Prayer
Jonathan Fletcher

The way he lies more than the Devil,
the way he talks about the stranger,
the way his policies treat the widow and the orphan,
the way he sells the Gospel for $59.99,
my fingers tighten as if for prayer.
But I can't make myself pray for him.
Did Jesus bless Pilate or Herod?
I'm sometimes more Roman than Christian.
I'm sometimes more Old Testament.
Forget the ploughshares, forget *Matthew 5:44*.
Give me a helmet, spear, and shield.
Fingers to fist, fist to sword,
sword to sword, me a sword.
And yet, I can't forget you, Peacemaker.
Or the way they made you one with wood.
Or the way you leaked water and blood.
Or that your fluid was for him as much as me.
O Lord, help me turn nothing crimson.
But from now until he's out of office,
let me be as direct as a nail.
Let me be firm as a hammer.

Another View
Danilah De Los Santos

I saw her, like I always do,

Looking radiant, as I first knew.

Oblivious, never seeing what she means, Veiled by the crowd, lost in their schemes. Even if she'd glimpsed, she'd never be the same, Devastated, as she dimmed her flame.
Youthful once, decaying in the rain,

Overwhelmed in her pain.

Underlying with regret, I see in her eyes, Diminishing hope, she still denies. Elegant still, she wears a disguise,

All while her spirit slowly dies.

Resilient she stands, though fragile within. At last, I wish to see her grin
The storm that bubbles inside

Lurking to strike just as an ocean tide Earthquakes as natural as they come
Are all reckless, random as any other scum Special it is, to see such a site
To see, how they put up a fight

But do they really see a disaster?

Even amongst never considering other factors Factors that pain us to understand
Overviewing as it all expands

Rewinding the time when nothing was guaranteed Evening comes, another view we see

My name is greater than I feel
Ben Salinas

Benito
Spanish version of Bénédict
Formed from the latin words for "good" and "speak"

Well spoken.

Juarez, then Mussolini

Benito the Great
Benito the Dictator

But also,

Benito Corghi
Long-distance truck driver
shot by an East German border guard
while crossing to get certificates he forgot.
Benito the absent minded

Benito Sr
Model immigrant second,
something ineffable first.
Turned funds earned working fields
into a college degree.
I understand him more now but only slightly.
Benito the father

Benito Jr
I'm ambivalent towards him.
He is wiser now and therefore more unsure.
Some combination of good luck and average genes.
Not great, not terrible

maybe honorable, mostly capable.
Benito the son

I am neither here nor there,
but somewhere, waiting.
Waiting for history to do with me what it will.

To Those Whose Blood Soaks the Holy Land
Adela Najarro

The women. The girls. That one girl
in the video with blood-stained
pajama bottoms, pushed and shuffled
into a vehicle. Too many lost
the ability to breathe. Too many lost
the integrity of their bodies. They lost
their father's protective shawl,
their mother's comforting prayers.
May God's gentle touch rest
on wounded shoulders,
smooth the wrinkles from rumpled shirts,
remove knots from disheveled hair,
shine light through the darkness
of underground tunnels.
Forgetting is also a form of hope—
the mind's resolution
to survive. May they forget
the touch on skin,
that skin tearing, those who tore
into their undoing.
Not only a few.
So many girls, sisters, daughters, wives,
friends—all deserve
open doors, to step onto patios,
walk on sidewalks, laugh.
Outside, the midday heat
radiates over a burning sea.

The People of the Valley
Carlo R. Guinita

Underneath the two troughs of mountain
Where river drawn with smooth edges in between
The leaves of greenery ruffles as the wind blows the field
While crops turn to golden yellow on its yield
Cloudless sky hovers atop the blue horizon

When the air feels all humid
And it set sail in opposite direction
Dark clouds begins to cover over the valley
Rain dazzles at the top of the fertile soil
Planting season starts to recall

When the lushes of all greens started to frown
And the air is being left empty from the scorching crown
Warm and bright all throughout sunny days
The land thirsts even for a single drop of rain
Water is reverted from the river for a generous gain

When the sky is painted with golden yellow
And its mirage becomes the springfield on its hue
Crops are ready to settle into the deep silo
Sickles and daggers flung to the field away from their saddle
Harvesting season seems to be bountiful as heard by their loud giggles

Farming has its rhythm by the tune of the wind
The farmers of the valley with the heights of the alpine
Long generation of culture, they have become intertwined
Even if books are seldom in their town
Their own story with the wind and the sky never let them down

In the future near, there was a phenomenon rare
The rain comes in the least as it is expected
The drought takes longer than it should be
It seems like the sky and wind had betrayed them
There must be reason beyond their valley they need to redeem

The people of the valley climb the top of the mountain
In search for the knowledge outside of their ridge
They witnessed the stonewalls with loud noises and fiery lights
The wind and the sky had found new acquaintances
In their wonder, they have solve their mystery

Tail of a Blind, Three-Legged Dog
Hayden

(A Reverse Poem)

What light we can find when the world seems to be burning
When the Vet found him in a ditch in Mexico
We don't know if he had a name or a home
On a starless night stretched into dusky morning
Before a black thread could be distinguished from white
We don't know who or what shattered his back leg and jaw
Every single day, for three months he held on
Distressed vets resigned each morning that he may not make it
They realized there was no chance
To save the limb or exiled eyesight
It's a fool's errand and none of it really matters anyway
Never believe
"There is a chance this could work out."
"You can make a difference in the world."
Many would agree
"It's just a dog after all."
"Just put him down."
"You can't save them all."
how many said
It's heartbreaking to imagine
His joyous, thumping tail, goofy grin, collar's jovial jingle
Stroking his shiny charcoal coat
Fingertips reading his halfmoon shaped leather scars
scattered across his skin in constellations
What hope is left to engage with
In this often dim and unsettling world

Read in reverse, from bottom to top, for a different perspective.

El Valor de Dos Personas

Victor Benavides

Aquí en el Valle,
practicamos las dos idiomas,
Nuestros padres nos dicen,
Que es el valor de dos personas,

We tend to switch
from English to Spanish,
In short conversations,
poems or language,
We speak without thinking,
a pocho type Spanglish,
We tend to speak it proudly,
Como? - ya lo sabes.

The first of november
Julia-Paz

Sometimes I lose my drive to exist.

It comes randomly, yet suddenly.

I will crave to melt into my bed or to stare off

into the sky and disappear for a while.

My phone goes off and I'll silence it,

leaving it on my desk as I run off to avoid expectations. Existing is so
hard most days.

I still can't believe that I've been existing

for all these years without you.

And I like to believe, "but I'm doing it!"

But am I?

Am I actually living my life even though you're no longer here? I wake up, I eat,
I shower, I work.

I watch TV and read books.

I laugh, but it hurts sometimes.

And boy do I cry.

I'm existing, clearly.

These words didn't just manifest on the page.

I've written them here.

I pray about these words.

I think about them and I drag them through time and space. From mind
to paper, to lips to a mic.

I create, therefore I exist, right?

Love and Satisfaction at the Roach Hotel
Jeff Woodruff

Saturday, December 14, 2024
6:02 PM

We have visitors in the night
They break bread with us
Like people, I guess,
They are our guests
We are generous hosts
We are the roach air b and B
We leave crumbs
Like Hansel and Gretel
they follow to the futon
On our guest room
We have prepared for
Their entourage
To share our Southern Hospitality
They like watermelon and love.
They have all been to the third grade
And know how to multiply

Soul-house
Bill Mainous

awake inside a city under siege
i'm among a perishing populace

a trench of bullet-shattered windows
network of wasteland a fallen metropolis
you know this since we barely survive
we sleep without water or warmth

in café ruins you discuss literature
we imagine drinking lattes pausing
only to complain about the staff

living in high cotton
as the old timers might say

been awhile since getting
bombed out of our minds

seems sunshine is only temporary like
a brief cameo that comes and goes too soon

still through all this my good friend
my heart knows the death of death

Tears falling from my eyes
Aldo Cristian Méndez Castillo

After the dark, a tear fall,
Secret poem I try to write,
Somehow pain is still there,
I don't remember, I don't care.

Dreams shatter around me,
Hard to tell which piece it is,
However, a promise remains,
Something I loved, and left.

Another piece of sorrow falls,
I remember her name, her smile,
But now, I am just an empty shell,
A shadow of a man, a crying one.

The winter begin to fill my life,
A white prison made by myself,
Still, I know someday it will end,
I will wait patiently, I won't cry.

Park Hill Remembered
Trevor Wainwright

It was a place of work, hazardous to health
While for its owners it brought in much wealth
Then came nationalisation taken over by the nation
Toiling underground cousins and brothers,
Fathers, sons and many others
Shaft 1 took the men down the hole
Shaft 2 equipment and brought up the coal
Workshops with tradesmen all knowing
Maintained the machines and kept the pit going
Lamproom staff kept the lamps bright
For those that worked in the mines perpetual night
Pit top locos small and stunted wagons of coal they moved and shunted
In the screens time seemed to drag
Watching the coal pass and removing the slag
Working there for many an hour
The end of the shift and a welcoming shower
Now only memories remain of Park Hill's story
The land restored to nature's glory

*Park Hill was a coal mine situated to the East of the city of Wakefield in what was
then The West Riding of Yorkshire where I worked for three years from Mar 1967 – Jul
1970 from the age of 15 to 18 It closed down in 1983 and the surrounding land was
turned into a nature reserve. After I wrote this poem I went and recorded it on video
showing what the land is now like.*

Katman Ken
Trevor Wainwright

As a strike it was my first not the best or the worst
To a meeting we went as a man to see if things were going to plan
It seemed to go well until the moment when
They asked any questions up stood Sparky Ken
Saying "when we talk of support I know who will need it
there's a cat at that pit, who's going to feed it?"
Someone made a speech he'd got it off pat
Only for Ken to stand and say "who's going to feed the cat?"
A door opened and there rolled out two men trying to knock each other out
Neither the upper hand could gain and so rolled back in again
Then four men went off for a game of skat
And Ken stood up again and said "who's going to feed the cat?"
Others talked and drank their beer before it went flat
And Ken continued to stand up and say "who's going to feed the cat?"
The meeting was becoming quite at task
Cos' "any questions?" someone did ask
Well hit me with a bat
Cos' Ken stood up again and said "who's going to feed the cat?"
That was all in the past and the pit didn't last
Me and Ken went our separate ways but I remember those striking days
And to Ken I'll take of my hat
For the times he stood and said "who's going to feed the cat?"

Cat's were originally used at coal mines and kept the stables clear of mice and rats in the days of pit ponies in return they received food, shelter, water and care from the miners. There was still one at Park Hill when I worked there, Ken was an electrician (Sparky) who used to look after it. We went on strike in 1969 and Ken was worried about the cat so brought the subject up at a union meeting.

I always tell everyone you died

Sandra Arenas

"Where is your friend?"
"Oh, I lost them last year," I tell them.
people always assume that to lose
means death and not to lose
someone in indifference
> in distance
> in insurmountable changes of character
> in fights fought in silence
> in unsent texts
> in forgetting birthdays
> in assuming I'm not trying my best
> in assuming your thoughts.

I always tell everyone you died
because that way it is easier to let you go
because that way it means death took you
because that way it means you didn't decide to leave
me.

I put candles on your made-up grave
where I pray made-up prayers,
begging the god you don't believe in to let you rest in peace.
Maybe god saved you from the hell we built
by accident.

So why am I still burning?
Do you miss me in that imagined heaven of mine,
where I see you swim in the river Lethe?
You never learned to swim.
I pray the current doesn't carry you too far.

But you exist without
> me,
and I'd rather
> die.

d i s t a n c i a

Sandra Arenas

anhelo sentirme cerca.
no se puede si llevo la distancia
en los huesos.

rostros ausentes
miradas que no se estrellan.

niego encontrarme en reflejo
espejo en otro.

habito la duda
consumo mi propio eco
me vivo en ardor constante
por otro.

no quiero otro.
otro se va.
yo me quedo.

Cruzar
Emmanuel Con Dos Emmes

Inhala.

Exhala.

Apaga la radio. Quítate los lentes. Baja las ventanas. Prepara documentos. Avanza. Inhala.

Exhala. Saluda. Da tu VISA y pasaporte. Siempre da el pasaporte. Ignora cuando te reclamen diciendo que no debes dar el pasaporte. Recuerda, algunos te reclaman cuando no lo das. Sé cordial. Respetuoso. «¿De dónde vienes?», «¿a qué vienes?», «¿con quién te vas a quedar?», «¿en dónde vive?», «¿cuándo te regresas?», «a ver tu boleto de regreso», «¿algo que declarar?», «¿cuánto dinero traes en efectivo?» Habla despacio. No levantes la voz. Responde cada pregunta. Tú sabes todas las respuestas. No titubees. Contacto visual. Inhala. Sé rápido. No tan rápido. No te pongas nervioso. No les des razones para darte el papel amarillo. No les des razones para mandarte al *cuartito*. Tienes todos los documentos necesarios a la mano. Y más, por si los necesitas. Exhala. Inhala. No te alteres. Exhala. No olvides que su estado de humor tiene tu futuro bajo su yugo. Ignora los gritos. No tiembles. Responde. Claro. Conciso. Inhala. Usa buen inglés, pero no tan bueno. Usa mejor español. Hazles entender que tienes una vida fuera del país. Que vas a regresar. Que esto es temporal. Exhala. Inhala. Ignora el alto volumen de su voz. Mantén el tuyo nivelado. No te rías. No hagas chistes. Solo ríete de sus chistes. Sé serio. No tan serio. «Da gracias que no te tocó una mujer», diría tu familia. Aunque sabes que aquí no hay diferencia de género. Todos son iguales. Tu futuro bajo su yugo. No menciones a tu familia. Solo a quien sea relevante. Dales información. No demasiada. No les des razones para más preguntas. Tu futuro depende de esto. No es la primera vez. No será la última.

«Pásale.»

Agradece. Toma tus documentos. Desea un buen día. Sube las ventanas. Avanza. Toma la curva. Lentamente. Sigue derecho.

Exhala.

Amor Felino
Emmanuel Con Dos Emmes

Oí tu voz en mi primera vida
Esperando
a que mi
nombre
llamara En
la segunda,
conocí
tu cara
Tremendo
oasis que
nunca se
olvida

Y fue
hasta mi
tercera
vez nacida
Que tu
aroma
al fin
mi nariz
gozará Es
prueba de
que nada
nos separa
Esta
existencia
cuádruple
vivida

Fue en la
quinta que

alcancé a
asimilar
Tu matiz,
saturación y
contraste Seis
momentos
en los que yo
exclamé

Que tu
encanto no
tiene similar Y
aunque en mi
última vida me
dejaste Morí
grato porque
en todas te
amé

We Can Be a River

Ron Ramírez

Listening to the whispering wind I begin my life as a stream
The odds may be against me
For myself, I try to redeem

Glistening in the shimmering sun Running down a mountain slope Move
with courage across the earth With my heart filled with hope

Hammering with our blistering fists With time we begin to know
We can make our own way
Now we all can join the flow

Pampering with our clambering hands Only time will tell
Give our all until we die
Its ending with a quell

Guiding my path by shining stars My pulse becomes too weak
I sense the pain within my heart I can be heard, but do not speak

Lighting my way by brightening moon I start to become so tired
Although I have retained my faith I lack the strength required

Rage on to our restoration
Improve our integration
Victory is our validation
Empower our exploration
Recognize our representation We can be a river

I should be over it.

Rolando Serna

The idea that I did anything wrong.
The thought that I was a victim.
It never crossed my mind.
I was raised to be proud of fathering my son.
I was thirteen and she was twenty-one.
The next year I was the father of my son.
I should be over it, the Tio would cheer me on
Look at our nephew, he has grown up fast.
Holding down a job putting in hundred-hour weeks
I should get over it and I still do not understand.
Why was she treated like the victim?
When I was the younger of the two
It is never spoken about, and I thought I was ok.
Until my twelve-year-old son asked me if he was old enough
If I would take him to boys' town like his friends had gone
I should get over it until I realize it.
That he was too young to give consent, and I would never do that to him.
What my uncles did to me
I might not be over it.
The one thing I know is true.
The bullshit my uncles put me through
I will never do that to you.
The cycle of abuse that I was accustomed to too.
Will never be passed, my son.
From me to you.
I should be over it until I start to think.
This is why I do not trust my kids with anyone.
Child abuse is never ok.
I should be over it but just not today.

Baby shoes for sale, Never worn
Kemberly Borrego

Baby shoes for sale, never worn,
A story of dreams shattered and torn.
In a nursery once filled with hope's embrace,
Now echoes silence, an empty space.

Each tiny shoe, a tale untold,
Of promises made, now grown cold.
In a mother's heart, a longing deep,
For the child she held, but could not keep.

Glimpses of laughter, fleeting and faint,
In the whispers of wind, a mournful plaint.
A father's hands, trembling with grief,
Grasping memories that offer no relief.

Baby shoes for sale, a heartache profound,
In each stitch and lace, love tightly wound.
They speak of a future, now lost in the mist,
Of a tender soul, too soon dismissed.

For every step that was meant to be taken,
A path now deserted, dreams forsaken.
In the stillness of night, their absence mourned,
Baby shoes for sale, never worn.

En los Momentos Finales
Kemberly Borrego

En los momentos finales, cuando el tiempo se detiene,
y la brillante llama de la vida se apaga lentamente,
dicen que la mente toca su última melodía,
mostrando recuerdos amados una y otra vez.

Y en esos siete minutos, mientras los pensamientos fluyen,
a través de escenas felices que mi alma retuvo,
sé que ustedes, mi familia, llenarán ese espacio, con sus sonrisas, su amor y su
cálido abrazo.

Cada risa compartida, cada palabra susurrada, en esos instantes
preciosos, todo será recordado. Ustedes son mi alegría, mi canción
más dulce, el refugio donde siempre mi corazón pertenece.

Cuando el tiempo regrese a momentos puros, al amor que construimos,
tan fuerte, tan seguro, serán la luz que brille en mis ojos al cerrar,
el último destello antes de dejarme llevar.

Veo sus rostros en cada escena querida,
el amor que vivimos, los lugares de mi vida.
Serán mi calma, mi paz final,
en esos fugaces instantes, su abrazo inmortal.

Cuando los recuerdos inunden, suaves y sinceros, sepan que mis últimos
pensamientos serán eternos. Porque en esos siete minutos, mi corazón
hallará el amor y la calidez que siempre me acompañará.

Y cuando llegue ese momento, como sé que llegará, cuando mi mundo
se apague y todo quede en paz, ustedes serán la esencia de mis sueños
finales, las estrellas que guiarán mis destellos celestiales.

Rio Bravo Blues

Reyes Cárdenas

My little girl gets tangled in the razor wire
the panic in her eyes pains me in the dark

I can hear the water rush against the wire
faraway faint lights bristle and a dog barks

slowly and nervously I try to untangle her
I keep an eye on the river's edge

" Please hurry, papi." she cries softly
our world hangs on a steep ledge

the razor wire tears her dress
but to me it has torn her flesh

I hate myself but I have no other choice
I thought only my country had no heart

we crawl onto the muddy river bank
we keep our heads down and breathe

we keep low and hide in some brush
" Papi, I'm scared.' she tugs at my torn sleeve

Jaime
Edward K Gonzales

He gave me my first pocket knife
I was shown fields of nopal and tuna
From which we assembled salsa
From there we hung a left which led to
A long forgotten vineyard
After acquiring our booty we transported home
To commence squeezing to juice
And jarring to jelly
He was fundamental to my learning
To prepare many foods to tamale to posole
And a mean French toast
Besides the fact my mother instructed me
To keep him at arm's length
As she said was uncle not dad
A major deception
He was truly my dad

Ponce

Mariana Mcdonald

21 de marzo de 1937
Dia amargo, sangriento.
Domingo de Ramos al sur,
cielo de estrella y azul.
Por los siglos el lamento.
Olor a sangre en el viento,
tiemblan huesos en el Bronze.
¡Fuego bestial! Entonces,
¡Muertos! Almas inocentes,
que siembran almas conscientes.
Siempre recordemos Ponce.

Décima pa' la Caminata
Mariana Mcdonald

De costa a costa por Oscar
caminan en la verde luz,
banderas de estrella y cruz.
Tráelo a casa es el cantar,
Trae el día que él verá el mar.
La senda dura, no siempre grata,
siguen aunque duelen patas.
Con firmeza del guayacán,
demuestran valor con afán.
¡Por Oscar, la caminata!

Emmy Pérez in Flight
Tom Murphy

Emmy Pérez writes a poem.
Journal in hand with poem pen

Consults her phone for phrases.
Maybe Emmy Pérez writes notes

on her students' work: suggests
enjambment. Emmy Pérez

steadily arranges words on the page,
journal flat on the tray table

where the flight turbulence
impedes Emmy's graceful pen stroke

air pocket hard smacks
ink askew, Emmy's breath

draws in the N95 black mask
heart leaps as hand scribes

into Houston, "Poets
going down in flames."

Todos mundo caos;
air current quality atmospheric

rivers — winds of Jupiter
pen in hand, one more flight home

en el Valle, Rio Grande.
Emmy Pérez duels through duende.

Southern Gothic, El Paso
DUGGAN

It's hot enough here
for fruit to swell
and sweat
and insects to feed
on the beads.

Heat like tinnitus -
a buzzing malice
weighting the air -
the weather meaner
than the proceeds of a church plate.

A saggy-bottomed cat,
toothless and
orange as a sage fire,
limps towards the shade
nursing thoughts of murder

while the sun
pounds its fists
on each man and his dog,
causing strays of both kinds
to stumble on rock-hard mud -

on dust and shale
with flint-sharp edges -
on rusty dreams
burned clean of hope
like a long-repented tattoo.

A veces…
José Luis Moreno

A veces tengo en mi pecho
una parvada de aves
como primavera eterna
no quieren salir de viaje
y románticas anidan
por temor de deslumbrarme
y titilan por mis ojos
sus brillos como diamante.
Hay veces que alguien los mira
y les asusta el enjambre,
de tantas plumas azules
rebotando en los cristales
de mis ojos que parecen
un gran mundo en soledades.
Otros dicen que son flores
o las ramas de los árboles
que guardan en sus contornos
a los San Pedro salvajes
y entre llamas desgarradas
hay pájaros color sangre
que volando entre bandadas
forman una bella imagen
del amanecer eterno
con la luz de muchos ángeles.
A veces se asoman tanto
como un infierno fragante
y se escapan de mi boca
recitando sus paisajes
plasmándose en mi cuaderno
sus palabras invernales
miedo tengo de tenerlas
por mi corazón que late

porque parecen corceles
que salen por todas partes
haciendo temblar mi pecho
que valiente los combate.
Hay veces que son tan rosas
con hermosas claridades
viniendo con tantos sueños
y con olor a azahares
parecen las primaveras
esas que fueron de antes
donde encontraba esperanza
y el refugio de mis aves
en mi cuaderno se lucen
como los bellos romances.

Balada de la redención
José Luis Moreno

Al mismo cielo y a mi Dios sublime
sin más aviso les pedí consuelo,
la tarde sin querer estaba muerta,
y triste mi alma se vistió de invierno.
¿Por qué se tiene que morir la gente?...
¿Por qué los cielos me parecen negros?...
toda mi angustia se vistió de luto
cuando en su frente le dejé mi beso.
No pude ver de nuevo sus pupilas
ni al ángel blanco que veló su sueño...
sentí tan solo el palpitar de un ave
como el crujir de ramas en el fuego.
Y le grité al señor, con mi tristeza,
y le grité con mi agotado pecho:
¿Dónde es que estas señor? ¿Se fue tu amor?
Tan solo en su respuesta vino un viento...

y como sombra me quedé en silencio.
El viento perfumó la triste estancia,
nadie pudo notar, en su dolor,
orlados ángeles batir sus alas.
Se vieron maravillas en el cielo
al rasgar los querubes lindas arpas.

Entonces puse al suelo mis rodillas
y puse en manos de mi Dios su cuerpo
y en el concilio de mi triste pena,
se asoma de mi alma... Padre nuestro
que estás en el…

Despedida

José Luis Moreno

El mar reclama todo, y mis cenizas
volaron de tu mano aquella tarde
el triste firmamento ya no arde.
Ni tú, con tu mirada lo matizas...

El viento me ha llevado enamorado
por mares, montes, valles y colinas
volé con mil hermosas golondrinas
que libre soy de un cuerpo tan cansado.

Mas mi alma triste vuelve sin consuelo,
tu fuiste la tormenta embravecida
y en un relámpago me diste vida
y has quedado sin luz mirando al cielo.

No quiero que me busques por las flores
ni dejo en mil aromas todos esos
humores que se sienten como besos
y no estoy ni en el aire, ni en rumores.

Y si sientes de nada escalofrío
es solo neurastenia que importuna.
No me busques amor ni por la luna
ni en la canción que tararea el río.

Si encuentras la mañana sucia en nubes
verás que por los montes crece vida,
entonces sentirás mi despedida
en canto de chicharras y querubes.

La tarde mortecina como broche
te acordará de mí, las alegrías.
De luz se llenarán las sombras mías
que un ángel me encamina en esta noche.

No volverán

José Luis Moreno

Volverán las oscuras golondrinas
—Gustavo Adolo Becker

Me siento como nunca... triste, en ruinas.
mi piel se mira seca y cuarteada
¿Volverán las oscuras golondrinas
a su casa que espera abandonada?
Mis ojos con un dejo amarillento
miran que escapa el tiempo solitario.
Tan solo me consuela el viejo viento
y las perlas oscuras de un rosario.
Mis lágrimas escapan a la tierra,
mi mente escucha voces como en coro
y estando en esta soledad que aterra,
mi corazón repica más sonoro.
Con esta depresión es todo denso,
mas busco terco en mis memorias frías
que escapan hacia el cielo, como incienso,
como las horas y también los días.
La pena que se aferra y se levanta,
me llena el cuerpo y alma con dolores.
Siempre pido a la imagen de una santa,
aquella que a Juan Diego dio sus flores,
milagros para un cuerpo desgarrado
que vió del cielo siempre maravillas
y al mundo como a todo a respetado
mas siente por su pecho mil astillas.
Me miro en el espejo cual el muro,
sin pintura y con polvo se reviste
y siempre muy callado y más oscuro
que en la bóveda de una tumba triste.
La parda golondrina no se atreve

a sofocar la soledad, que advierte,
no vuelve a dar la paz aún tan leve,
que viene a dar el ángel de la muerte...
Soy un páramo lóbrego y sombrío
que en aras tiene toda fe desierta.
Soy la noche que vive del hastío,
soy la voz que cantando vive muerta,
las penas que de viejas ya no gimen.
Ya que ninguna golondrina alcanza
a rebajarse al tenebroso crimen
de aquella con sus besos de esperanza.

Because of the Refusal
Christopher T. Dabrowski

The Third World War started. Death decided she was fed up.

Her scythe tired her, and given the amount of work, she decided that a lawnmower would be more useful. Yet, the Earth Affairs Ministry declined her funding.

Under these circumstances, Death, called the Grim Reaper erroneously because she was a woman, although it was not apparent, decided to end her cooperation with the Creator.

When she returned home, she looked at herself in the mirror.

Um, I'm not getting old – she thought. – Maybe I should become a model? I could be on the album cover of some metal band.

The Sins of the Family
Jennifer Villegas

Broken parents breed broken men and women.

Men who rage at the moon after too many libations have gone down his gullet. Speaking to

ghosts of the past and begging for forgiveness. Rosy cheeked and eyes like rubies.

Women who grew cold and could not give love, resentment brewed and could not be hidden, so

a house never became a home.

The inebriation of life's ebb and flow. Sunken in lament, broken mothers and fathers whose

children sink into the same liquid libations and mend others until they break. Men and

women who find solace in numbness and in strangers arms.

Liquor blurs the faces and lightens remembrance of the search for love that was expected

in adolescence but never received, waging wars inside themselves no one can see and they

do not dare to speak. Because you don't mention those types of subjects.

The children are not okay.

October 31,2018

EL CANTO DEL COYOTE Y EL SOL

Demian Palacios

El tiempo se llevó al sol
con el canto de los años tristes,
ya no caen plumas en el aire.

Donde todo se hacía lluvia,
un colibrí de madera que se hace nube
y la diosa luna carga un conejo de noche.

Los días se mueven en piedras bajo el agua,
la vida nace con las primeras formas,
que surgen en las hojas verdes
y las hojas amarillas que tienen las tardes del sol.

El camino de las estrellas pasa con el canto
de la piedra blanca,
las palmas sonando con el canto verde
de un quetzal.

En este cerro de los astros
un coyote escupe al sol,
y el sol a la tormenta de la luna
y el centro de flores cubrirá el pantano.

Sobre las piedras se levantan las nubes
que van de una montaña al mar,
dentro de la peña viven los muertos
y los seres nacen semilla.
Para que el viento nos acerque
agua del cielo,
será mejor un canto de noche,
un aposento y un ave que cante
con la voz de las flores.

A SIETE DÍAS SE OCULTA EL SOL

Demian Palacios

Cedan los terrenos del agua
o los suelos santos,
suras de una meca
certezas de dichos de Muhámmad

Él hizo salir de sus hogares
la aleya de la usura y del hambre;
traerá la guerra de Alá,
a siete días donde se oculta el sol.

Hashem espera que caigan las mezquitas,
vuelve con malas artes al mundo en la ceniza,
el silencio se escucha en el valle del Nilo
con apelaciones de muertos sin nombre.

Él es el eterno que vuela sobre los cuerpos,
y otros piden refugio por debajo de la arena;
venimos al paso de los reyes a Jerusalén
peregrinando estrellas del cielo.

Ya no huele,
ni saben como antes el falafel y el hamin,
con voz tranquila, se repite el llanto
que han puesto las noches sobre la luz.

Nos han guiado a este lugar sin rumbo
los mensajeros no trajeron la verdad:
solo querían restos en las cruces,
nos hicieron de barro
nuestra claridad se va en la luz del alba.

Entre sueños y realidad
Edgar Salazar

El ver tus ojos y tu sonrisa
La primera vez que escuché tu risa
Cuando estábamos juntos y el tiempo iba a prisa
Oh el beso de la playa mientras nos sopló la brisa

Te observe de lejos y me quise acercar
Mis palabras se ahogaban intentaba gritar
Una última vez te quería abrazar
Suena la alarma es hora de despertar

Aveces me siento mal estoy en sismo
Me lanzó al vacío y a su abismo
Te extraño aunque ya no somos los mismos
En el calor de tu pecho descansaba de mi mismo

Eh estado pensando mucho en ti últimamente
Mi sonrisa me mienta cuando me miro al espejo
Alzo mi copa cada luna creciente
Y en vez de olvidarte amplifico mis complejos

De-culo-nizacion Is Not A Metaphor

Featured Poet: Tezozomoc

"...we want to be sure to clarify that decolonization is not a metaphor. When metaphor invades decolonization, it kills the very possibility of decolonization; it recenters whiteness, it resettles theory, it extends innocence to the settler, it entertains a settler future. Decolonize (a verb) and decolonization (a noun) cannot easily be grafted onto pre-existing discourses / frameworks, even if they are critical, even if they are anti-racist, even if they are justice frameworks."

—Eve Tuck and K. Wayne Yang: "Decolonization Is Not A Metaphor"

It's not enough
that you and I,
have to teach community.

That we are
truly more civilized,
more adapted hygienically,
to the land
more adapted to
the hypocritical oath
of our colonizer.

That we have
always bathed
before the face of poverty.

We have been up
with the cold concrete.
Alone with
Santa Ana Iron Maidens.

Amongst the morose
and soul destructive WASP cells,
Here, on the artificial landscape.

{Pause}

My epidermis
is wanting shelter
from your eugenic delusions.
Fellow inhabitants
you have peeled
the white hood
and now we can deal
with your schism,
with the broken "*bell curve*".

Hey, Hey, Hey!

Our ancestors
left with
well articulated
demands for life,

"You think the creator,
sent you here
to dispose of us
as you see fit.
If I thought
you were sent by creator,
I might be induced
to think you had a right
to dispose of me.

Do not misunderstand me,
but understand me fully
with reference to my affection
for the land.

I never said the land was mine
to do with as I choose.
The one who has a right to dispose of it
is the one who has created it.
I claim a right to live on my land.
And accord you the privilege to return to yours.

Brother we have listened to your talk.

And my people have called upon me
to reply to you." by *Chief Joseph, Nez Perce*

Because it is not enough
that we were born
on the San Joaquin Valley by
the gentle Sierra Madre slopes.
Or on high Zapotec Sierras,
or the coastal lands
were **Xipe Totec** had
lent his liberating path.

Born in the barrios
of the **Kumi Vit**[1], La Desgraciada Reina
de los tolºnºliztli, los Pobres.
Motolºnia
Motolinia, we suffer, we suffer.

On this landscape of incarnate dreams
where '...our skin
aches with the loss
of Colorado, the loss of flat plains,
the deep ravines of New Mexico.

Where our skin is scoured
between black and white shades
of tan called brown,
stained by Arizona Sun,
dried by Texas winds
and frozen by Montana cold.

That our father's father laid track
from East to West
and Mictlampa to Huitzinahua,
criss-crossed these lands of ours.

That our men and women,

---

1   This is Los Angeles' Indigenous name. Kumi Vit natives who settled along its banks 1,500 years
ago called the "Pwinukipar--It is full of water."

their faces weathered by
cold and heat,
picked the fruit and
harvested the wheat
while our children
ate corn meant only for cattle.

America has grown
strong on our backs,
but remains weak
on the brims of all the,
main streets.'[2]

We have
erected civilization
with community at the center
in valleys where life seemed
impossible.

Where we were divided
against each other.
through race,
through economics,
through spiritual rape,
through cultural suicide,
But then through belief
and labor were,
again united.

It is not enough
Julio Cano --12 dies
because you feel
your real estate is losing value.

Where you have
equated homeowner associations with KKK,
Humanity with real estate,

---

2   Partial credit of this goes to the Whittier College Chicano Manifesto that was shown by the LA
Times with Martin Ortiz. on Nov. 11/13/94

ecology with Jim Crow,
nativism with race,
Isolation with success,
Armed security with serenity,
and greed with **prop. 187**.

It is not enough
that a boy named Gus
calls his big brother
at midnight Nov. 9
and says, "What's going to happen
to our little sister."

We are good keepers
of the land;
of our communities
of our children,
we keep our elders
at home and ask them
for their wisdom,
honor them
for the salvation they have
brought.

That we infuse
this decaying city,
with life,
with vision,
with compassion,
with hope,
with salvation,
with our powerful art;
that lives in our hearts,
murals, cars, and beyond
3 billion dollar mausoleums.

When is it enough?
I ask you, when?
When will we accept
that we will never be "white enough",

that we will never be sterile enough,
that we will never "be your kind of Americans",
because America is a big continent?

Please remind them,
"How many times must we burn the wagons,
before they understand."

The Slippery Semiotic Subject
Featured Poet: Tezozomoc

Dispatch: 10-4 (Roger, understood),
all units.
We have a 10-96 (Mental Subject),
requesting an APB for subject,
vague, shifting;
endowed with ambiguous signifier,
stemming primarily
from the academic division of labor.

The suspect is wanted
for questioning
in connection
with a series of 415s (disturbances).

If you see the suspect,
Please do not approach.
Call in immediately.
The suspect's aliases are:
the grammatical subject,
the legal subject,
the literary protagonist,
or the subject of history.

Be wary of the abstract,
transcendental subject,
with genealogy
to Cartesian, Kantian, or Hegelian idealism.
Suspect alias as Descartes 'ego cogitans',
Suspect alias as Kant's, "I think",
and Hegel's 'spirit'.

Dispatch: 10-4, all units.

Suspect is well known for
mystifying and illuminating
the mind of the proletariat.

Suspect operates by establishing
through constant collectives,
abstract or mythical subjects:
with nation,
state and class,
Spirit, and History.

Unit 1: 10-4, dispatch. I'm en route.

Unit 2: 10-4, dispatch. I'm also en route.

Dispatch: 10-0. All Units. (Caution)
Suspect is highly interactive
between the abstract,
known as the individual
subject of philosophy.

Unit 1: Code 5 (surveillance).
Unit 1: Code 2 (Urgent).
Dispatch, is this the Subject of theory?
The semiotic interaction between
the individual and the collective?

Dispatch: Unit 1. 10-4
Unit 1,
No, This is the slippery social subject
of linguistic context;
the subject of narrative programs
and discourse,
the infra- individual, individual,
artificial and supra individual actor.

Unit 2: Code 5 (surveillance).

Dispatch Code 2(Urgent).
Is this is the subject of 'disappearance'
the stereotype which diverts attention
from fact, that nobody is actually
able to define?
Who or what is exactly
about to disappear
or has already disappeared?
The subject that distinguishes
notions we can do without
from those that remain indispensable?

Dispatch is this the subject of anticipation,
the reconciliation
or the universal subject?

Dispatch: 10-4. Code 2.
Unit 2, this is the intellectual subject,
that causes difficulties,
the grammarian subject
with personal pronouns,
"i", "you", "he", "she", and "it".

The illusive subjectivity
of grammatology,
performative anthropomorphological
agent of pragmatics
that enumerates
unavoidable philosophical concepts.

The residual after image
of what doesn't disappear,
continues to pre-condition
meaningful speech,
speech on disappearance:
the self-reference of the 'I',
the subject as individual

consciousness of cognition,
the legal subject
the moral subject of sense,
the communicative 'I',
as a point of shared discourse,
of human life.

Dispatch: 10-4. All Units.
The suspect's call sign is:
Whiskey Tango Foxtrot
If you see the suspect,
please call in immediately.

Additional Information:
The suspect is believed
to be armed and dangerous,
considered to be a flight risk.
If you see the suspect,
do not approach,
call dispatch immediately.

Metadiscourse
Featured Poet: Tezozomoc

> *A famous pianist described the rules of his art. One must play, he said,*
> *exactly what is written on the score. Then doubting the truth of what he*
> *had said, "But what does 'exactly' mean?"*
>
> —*Michel Arrive*

Metadiscourse
is a fact of everyday life.

This is not an illusory bait
for coherence and comprehension.

The polysemic semiotic symbol
can produce three types of neurosis:
hysteria, obsession, and anxiety;
kind of like a homeowners association (hoa).

Language by its incompleteness
is a special social symbolic system.

Language, a two sided minion
conceived in the entrails
of materialism as the sign,
but pragmatically articulated
as a sanguine signified,
and stratifying signifiers.

Beyond the primal horde of
Kantian totalizing
linguistic imperialism
and its reductive-nativist
essentialism; that opposites
can subordinate and sublimate
under a unitary single object.

Something neurotics
with a simple
philological criticism
dispel as mirages.

The shackle chains of erasure
remove presuppositions
that language is the precondition
of the unconscious, but rather
the unconscious is a precondition
for linguistics.

The incorporeal signifier
sheds its stoic grounding
in the materialism
of the signified
and butterflies
ungrounded, empty,
lacking attachment.

The trickster cynical signifier
sometimes grasped as
an abstract entity;
gutteralized into phonemes;
maybe grasped as a concrete entity
once articulated into sounds.

The signifier of external perception,
the dominance of the letter,
the "order" word;
one as "ordering" the world,
and it doppelganger as "command";
its double discourse
as the discursive signifier,
the unconscious as discourse.

The strange simulacra
of language
is that it has no perceptible
entities at the outset,

yet it will not permit, nor doubt
they must exist
because they constitute it.
We bestow our mental health
on the faith of meta-language
the same regime of signification
that has rendered us
imperceptible at the onset,
but insists we exist
at some back alley
thrash strewn ghetto
syntagmatic transphasic
social domain;
some minor enunciative
muffled meta-discourse.

The antithetical existence
to remain locked
in the domain of meta-language,
always vulnerable
to the two antithetical signifieds;
none for which we have receipts.

Meta-discourse,
which must not be confused
by the trauma porn poet,
as the meta-language
of representation;
confronts us with a series
of processes which are ordered
in sequences
in which the word
must take its place.

If you are working
your trauma
don't get caught
in the linguistic game
of the reel.

The reel, in fact,
is attached by a piece of string to the child's hand,
the semiotic discontinuity,
the presence-absence, alternation,
the disappearance and returns.

Meta-language,
by making distant
or bringing closer the toy
which remains attached
lets us know
that it's master
of the situation.

[Conclusion of Anna O.]
Current research has suggested many illnesses which Pappenheim may have
had. Medical researcher Elizabeth Thornton, after interviewing many of Freud's
early patients, suggested that Pappenheim had tuberculous meningitis,[9]
a view supported by professor of psychology Hans Eysenck. Others have
suggested it was encephalitis, a form of brain inflammation.[10] Many have
also suggested that she suffered from a form of temporal lobe epilepsy since
many of her symptoms, including imagined smells, are common symptoms of
types of epilepsy.[11][8][10] According to one perspective, "examination of the
neurological details suggests that Anna suffered from complex partial seizures
exacerbated by drug dependence."[11]

Lejanía
Gabriela Iñiguez

De tanta filosofía,
llegue a la conclusión
que la mente no lo sabe
   todo.

De tanto pensar en las conclusiones,
di mil vueltas, y no escuche
el ocaso, ni las palabras de mi madre
a la hora del café.

Le di la vuelta, a mi presente
y a *chicotazos*, me devolvió
a mi regreso.

Aprendí, que un presente,
no llega dos veces,
y si, alguien me robo mi tiempo
fui yo, por no estar aquí.

Distance
Gabriela Iñiguez

After so much philosophy
I came to the conclusion
that the mind doesn't know
 it all.

After thinking so much of the conclusions,
I took so many turns, and I didn't listen
to the sunset, nor to the words of my mother
while drinking coffee.

I took a side turn on my present
and by *chicotazos*, I came back
to my beginning.

I learned, that a present,
doesn't arrive a second time,
and if, someone robbed me of my time
it was me, for not being here.

Direcciones en opuesto
Gabriela Iñiguez

Veo el árbol rumbo al este,
yo quiero ir al este,
escapar con sus ramas,
tocar su viento,
pero el este
quiere que me quede,
que escriba
y continué mi camino
con dirección al oeste.

All Was Silence
Jio De La Rosa

They dug too deep one might say. Instead of a Balrog they unleashed Ancestral Rage. The war started at home and quietly crept into the classroom. Fathers, brothers, husbands, uncles, friends. All voted against the women and girls in their lives. Brain dead hicks voted against their kin in the hopes of winning favor with the Putrid. Generational shame and racism bled out of the pores of the poorest demographic. The least educated. The most overworked. And the first to be slaughtered. The first to be sacrificed to Supremacy. What do you do when you realize that your community has turned against you? That they hate you so much they'll cut off their own limbs to eradicate you?

November 5, 2024. The End was Nigh.

When the polls closed, the chanting began, "Your body! My choice!" Ringing clear across a country no longer living under the illusion of Free. With a laborious sigh, the mountains cracked open. Fissures parted the roadways. The Big Oil coated maw of the Gulf swallowed the South in a rapturous gulp. The Deep claiming the lives of the Red, White, and Blue. Mother had had enough. She sent out the monsters of old. The slumbering beasts deep within the Earth's crust. Those she lulled back to bed whenever fracking roused them. Those she pacified when they polluted their waters. Sprites and fae and duendes bound by her spell, poured out on the world. Ravenous and without direction. With only a guiding instinct: la limpieza es salud. The sirens lured the sailors once again. Men desperate to pump their seed into anything with breasts nicer than their own.

Lloronas out for revenge. Looking for worthless m e n who believed themselves better than the nugget-shaped pink slime they ingested day and night. Women in White digging their claws into the hearts of those who coerce, who manipulate, who guilt into submission. Helping to soothe the hurt of the living. White women wearing blue bracelets cried as they watched the Men in their lives ripped limb from limb. Their end was met in the cleansing fire of the phoenix. Black, brown, indigenous women and femmes alike came together in a baptism of blood. La sangre de los hartos. One that washed away the pain of oppression. The weight of systemic racism. The inbred hatred that [many] colonizers carry. They washed away the need to educate others on why they should exist. Trans folk and queer folk and non-binary folk walked hand-in-hand. Working together to help the harpies, the ravens, the hags, the thunderbirds, the lobas, the leviathan, the angels, and demons all cleanse the earth of misogyny. Of patriarchy. Of self-obsessed m e n and w o m e n who only see their plight. Only feel their fear. Always choking on their false oppressions. Pick-me folk who live to complain.

To have to wear a mask is oppression. To tell them to fuck off is oppression. Break the nose of n a z i and they melt away under the consequences of their actions: "But my First Amendment right allows me to…," trickles from their mouths as blood ushers in their understanding. The Freedom to subjugate flows from them in rivers of regret. A fjord of fear and a tidal wave of ice-cold melted snow. To set a boundary to say no to ask not to be touched to walk alone at night or in broad daylight to be in our own homes living our lives going to work paying taxes raising our children to be better than us. Better than Them. A deep-seeded fear: for melanin kissed bodies to not only outnumber, but to out-class. They saw love and wanted to kill it. They saw acceptance and wanted to bleach it away. They saw hope and regurgitated hatred. They used a work of oral fiction to attack our Mother, and she finally had enough. The ancestors re-claimed their power and cleansed the earth of hateful, spiteful, useless, opportunistic sacks of human excrement. And all was silence.

Those that remained told stories of the Beginning in awed whispers. They never forgot the Rage they survived. The Rage they healed from. They led their lives, re-built communities, loved, cared, supported one another. They carried the message of their ancestors. They followed the guidance of Mother. They sacrificed the blasphemous at the first sign of dissent. Those who attempted to stoke the Old Fears. Those who refused to learn. Those who tried to resurrect the forsaken ways of a time long passed. "We are not going back." This is community. One free of fear. One free to live. To breathe. To bear children. To say no. To educate. To grow. To love.

In 10 years' time, the ancestors will resurface. They will crawl their way out from the depths of the Hell created for the w h i t e m a n. They will revel in the glory of what we have created from their demise. We have had enough. If you're reading this, you're one of the few who remain. Find comfort in knowing you are not alone. Remember to resist, always. Find hope in community. Love deeply and freely. And always know that you are not alone. The ancestors are watching, listening, guiding. Waiting.

BOUNDLESS YOUTH POETS

Cuando se fue

José González

Cuando se fue
nadie le ayudó
pero yo intenté.
Se le acabó la suerte
porque él no pudo
prevenir la muerte.
El hoyo que lo mató
a todos nos dañó.

Cuando se fue,
sus gritos no se escuchaban en la calle,
sino por todo el Valle.
Le gustaba caminar
y a veces correr sin parar,
pero nada de esto importaba
ahora que ya no estaba.
Siempre estará conmigo…

Cuando se fue
todos lo olvidaron
pero yo lo extrañé.
Quería que se quedara
con todo mi corazón,
y cuando dijo que yo lo iba amar para siempre,
tenía razón.
Abuelo, siempre lo recordaré.

José González is an 8th grader and is currently attending Ann Richards Middle School. José, in his free time likes to read about Greek mythology. He likes to write about the all powerful Greek gods like Zeus, Hades, and Poseidon.

For you, I'll try
Rocío Salazar

For you, I'll try
your tears I'll dry
your warm hands I'll hold
'til we both grow old

our problems we'll solve
'til like salt in water, we dissolve
and forever te amaré my love

Rocío Salazar is an 8th grader and is currently attending Ann Richards Middle School. Rocío in her free time likes to call her best friend. She likes to write about her best friend.

Ojos amables
Zulema González

"Los ojos marrones son feos."
Mucha gente dice esto,
pero yo nunca estaría de acuerdo,
y eso es por una razón especial.

It was because I loved his brown eyes,
I loved him from afar.
He was the first boy,
the first I cared for.

It all started when
one day he turned to me
and asked for a pencil.
Mesmerized by his brown eyes,
I couldn't look away.

Ever since then, we became so close,
even our teachers noticed.
He would win me prizes at the fair,
even though I wasn't ever there,
But he always said I was there spiritually.

He was the first boy to give me a Valentine's gift,
the first to give me a Christmas gift.
I remember being so surprised,
I just wanted to hug him,
but instead, I stared into his brown eyes.

I still remember March 14,
when he asked me, "May I be your boyfriend?"
That was the best day,
he was my first ever love.

I would walk around in his jackets,
he would hold my hand on field trips,
and he always looked at me with his cute brown eyes.

Zulema González, an 8th grader who is currently attending Ann Richards Middle School. She likes to shop, color, and play guitar in her free time. She likes to write about her life and struggles.

Getting Older

Paola Pachecano

I always think about what I use to say,
"I wish time went by faster."
Oh how I miss those days,
when I did not have a care in the world,
but now years pass like days.

It feels like I was just seven,
but I snap to reality and realize…
I'm now 14.
I now hear the whispers
and see the glares
that are like a burning beam.

I realize la vida no es perfecta.
En lugar de estar despreocupada,
ahora estoy ansiosa,
estresada,
celosa,
y ocupada.

Sometimes it feels like I'm trapped
in between two versions of myself.
One side of it is feeling
like the luckiest person in the whole world.
The other is feeling
like I have
no purpose,
no place in this world.

At times, life feels
meaningless and difficult,
like I'm trapped in a loophole,

feeling like everyday is the same thing
over and over again,
but it's all just part of getting older.

Paola Pachecano is an 8th grader and is currently attending Ann Richards Middle School. Paola in her free time likes to spend time with her family and play softball with her dad. She likes to write about personal experiences. In 5th grade, she wrote a sad poem about overcoming hardships.

A Trip I'll Never Forget
Joanna S.

The sweet aroma of chocolate
Flowing through the air.
A room filled with machines
mixing all at once
Sounding like a train next to my ear.

Riding on the bus,
going as fast as the wind.
Eating our snacks,
as we laugh and chat.
Screaming at each other
as we play puñetazo.

Stopping at a restaurant.
Leaving just as quickly as we entered.
Now arriving at the turtle sanctuary,
feeling like years have passed.
Seeing all the aquatic life
as we walked around for an eternity.

The sun beating down from the sky
as we enter the art workshop.
Carving a flower stamp,
making an ink painting,
and dying cloth with bright flowers.

The orange sky shining bright
as we enter the restaurant covered in plants.
Sitting with my friends choosing what to eat.
Ordering dessert as we talked.
Counting our money as we left.

Walking around the massive gift shop.
Spending my last 8 dollars on a Hello Kitty ring,
keeping it to remember this experience forever.

Joanna S. is an 8th grader and is currently attending Ann Richards Middle School. Joanna in her free time likes to draw, write, and listen to music. She likes to write about adventure, fantasy, and events based on real life experiences.

Stray Dog
Rubén Oviedo

I found you one the side of the road
You were dirty and you were scared
but I liked your hair
and the way
you wag your tail

you were small
and I was small

I took you home
and my parents and I showered you
You were beautiful

and your hair would shine
I named you Firuláis.
Now, you are mine .

Rubén Oviedo is a 7th grader and is currently attending Ann Richards Middle School. Rubén Oviedo in his free time likes to play football. He likes to write about love.

El perro fiel
Emmanuel G.

En la puerta del alma aguarda,
mirada que nunca falla.

Corre entre flores, sueña en olores,
su cola al viento, pura alegría.

De noche, callado guardián,
su pecho arde en lealtad.

Un amigo sin palabras,
pero todo su amor da.

Emmanuel G. is an 8th grader who is currently attending Ann Richards Middle School. He mostly enjoys writing about his pets, and spending his free time with his friends and family.

De día

Scarlett R.

De día me visita el sol.
De día se escuchan mis olas.
De día estoy fresca.

De día puedo sentir esa felicidad.
De día me visitan esas risas.

De día soy suave con mis olas.
De día también puedo ser fuerte.

De día me visitan las gaviotas.
De día los peces pasan sobre mí.
De día los caballitos de mar me visitan.

De día me mirarás bailando bajo el sol.

Scarlett R. is an 8th grader and is currently attending Ann Richards Middle School. Scarlett R. in her free time likes to paint. She likes to write about nature.

My definition of Love
Sofia Cuéllar

Love is affection, a soft feeling.
It is the spark of interest in something or somebody,
a warm attachment that seems like coming back home,
an unstoppable attraction.

Love is of many types.
There is an appreciation kind of love,
the emotional one that is like a flame.
There is the supportive love in money issues,
physical love built deep inside your heart,
and love that's formed in everyday help.

Love also moves through stages.
There's the falling in love,
the joy of discovering the good parts,
and the strength of building an attachment.

To me, love is to notice someone
and feel your whole world change.
It's a compassionate embrace of who they are.
And as for me, love does not need all the stages
It only takes one:
Capturing one 's corazón.

Sofia Cuéllar is an 8th grader and is currently attending Ann Richards Middle
School. Sofia Cuéllar in her free time likes singing, writing, reading, and
painting. She likes to write about love, nature, her feelings, and God.

Luna
Eliza Sánchez

I still hear the soft patter of your paws,
How you would run to greet me.
Your wagging tail and your kind, loving eyes.
You live in my heart now, not the skies.

We spent hours playing in the yard.
You made the hard days a little less hard.
At night, you would snuggle up next to me.
You were my home, my family.

Now the house feels too still and quiet,
And nothing can replace the space you filled.
I hope you're running in fields just as wide,
With stars and moon lighting your way.

I miss you, Luna, more than words can say.
But you're in my corazón every day.
You were my light, my true friend,
And my love for you will never end.

Eliza Sánchez is an 8th grader and is currently attending Ann Richards Middle School. Eliza Sánchez in her free time she likes to play volleyball. She likes to write about her dog.

My new guitar
Jerelyn Barrientos

I went to a music place
To find something to replace
As soon i enter
I walk to the center

A cold breeze struck at me,
like how the music flows on me.
Thinking i couldn't find nada
I found a classical guitarra

Whom the strings were stiff
There I would climb a cliff
The sound so strum
That makes me so dumb

Finally i made my mind,
But I think i have to find
Something new
Something old
Something I have for my own

Jerelyn Barrientos is an eighth grader and is currently attending Ann Richards Middle School. Jerelyn Barrientos in her free time likes to play sports. She likes to write about things that happen to her.

Confianza
Bianca Alvarado

Te conozco,
te ayudé cuando estabas triste
creí que podía tener fe en ti
creí que podía confiar en ti
solíamos hablar todos los días
pero ahora te sientes tan lejos.

Te lo he dicho todo
pero ahora todo eso está tirado
todo esto es solo algo aterrado
¿Por qué estás siendo así?
Quién diría que las palabras pueden ser tan hirientes
no sabía que serían tan sentimentales.

Es tan amable y fácil de abrirse
pero sin ti mi corazón necesita una puntada.
Es tan reflexivo y empático
nuestro argumento fue tan patético
pensé que podría tener fe en ti
realmente pensé que podía confiar en ti.

Bianca Alvarado is attending Ann Richards MIddle School in Texas as a seventh grader. In Bianca's free time, she likes to make paper stars and do diamond arts. Bianca is a smart, caring, and loving person. She looks forward to writing and publishing her own poems one day.

Lo que me pasó por culpa de mi alarma

Camila Elizondo

Cada noche ponía una alarma para las cinco cincuenta
para yo levantarme temprano
e ir a ver mis animales,
pero un día no sonó mi alarma
abrí mis ojos
y esperaba ver todo oscuro afuera,
pero ya estaba más que amanecido
eran las once
yo preocupada me levanté lo más rápido que pude,
mi mente nada más pensaba
que los caballos, perros, gallinas
y marranos estaban sin comer
y sin agua "pobres animales", yo pensaba.
Me sentí tan mal pero mañana me aseguraré
de poner mi despertador.
Lo que me pasó por culpa de mi alarma.

Camila Elizondo is a seventh grader and is currently attending Ann Richards Middle School. Camila in her free time likes to practice her poem for UIL.

Mi querida abuela
Norma Perales

Usted es la abuela perfecta
con hermoso pelo largo y chino
en un abrir y cerrar de ojos se lo corta,
cumpliendo una manda por su nieto.
Se mira en sus ojos café el amor que brinda.

Siempre está para todos día y noche
desde que el sol sale hasta que el sol se mete
le podemos decir "señora mil usos":
enfermera, abogada, maestra, son títulos sin certificados.

Hogar dulce hogar,
el significado que le dio a nuestra casa
donde nunca me faltó mi sopita de fideo
donde nunca me faltó el cuidado de mi abuela
donde nunca me faltó el amor
de mi querida abuela, mi lugar seguro.

Norma Perales is a 7th grader and is currently attending Ann Richards Middle School. Norma in her free time likes to write about her feelings and turn them into poems.

Love is a two way Mirror
Aaliyah Guerrero

El amor siempre será un espejo de dos vías. El amor puede fallar,
el amor puede tener éxito
y nunca sabemos cuál puede ser el camino.
El amor es un espejo de dos caras.
Así que sé feliz
con quién estés
nunca te enamores rápidamente
porque la confianza y los sentimientos
se pueden perder velozmente.

Aaliyah Guerrero is a 7th grader and is currently attending Ann Richards
Middle School. Aaliyah Guerrero in her free time likes to play school sports,
boxing, and working outside with farm animals. She likes to write about love,
family and heartbreaks.

Mañana no es para siempre
Felicity G.

"There may not always be tomorrow, so be grateful to everyone and everything you have."

—Anonymous

Por favor, no des por sentado tus días
Por favor, vive cada dia como si fuera el último
Porque el mañana no esta prometido
Y nunca sabes cuánto dura.

Time is precious although its not guaranteed
You will never know when your last day will be
Life is short, so do the best that you can
Cause it may not go according to plan
For tomorrow isn't promised
So please be grateful for the life that you have.

Agradece los dias que despiretas
Porque no todos tendremos esa suerte
Porque el mañana no esta prometido
Así que vive, ríe y ama.

So tell your loved ones how you feel
Cause life may seem oh surreal
For tomorrow isn't promised
Tell them now that you have the chance
Cause you never know what day will be your last.

Felicity G. is a 7th grader and is currently attending Ann Richards Middle School. Felicity in her free time likes writing poems. She likes to write about her brother or any ideas in her head.

Cáncer
Hailey Barrera

La peor cosa del mundo.
Se viene en los peores
momentos posibles.
a las personas más lindas y lindos.

Mi abuela no lo merecía.
Recuerdo los días
donde quería visitarte,
pero no podía.

Pensé que nunca te volvería a ver
la persona que más amé en el mundo.
Imaginé a Dios acogiendo a otro ángel en su cielo.
Durmiendo con el corazón pesado
solo pensando en ti.

Pero con Su gracia,
viviste para ver otro día.
Fui bendecida con otro día contigo.
Doy gracias a Dios por ti
todos los dias.

Te amo, abuela.

Hailey Barrera is a 7th grader and is currently attending Ann Richards Middle School. Hailey in her free time likes to practice guitar. She likes to write about her personal life.

Love for Basketball
April Badillo

Basketball
Is my favorite sport.
I dribble
Up and down
the court.
The ball goes up and
Down,
But when I lose the game
I frown,
The game is won with a team in mind.
We dribble, pass, and shoot
Until we win the hoop

April Badillo is a 7th grader and is currently attending Ann Richards Middle School. April Badillo in her free time likes to play Roblox. She likes to write about basketball.

Mom and Dad

Marven Rincon

Mom and Dad I love the way you love me
I love that you buy me whatever I want
but I hate they you guys get mad at me
 I love the way you guys are so kind
you guys are so generous to others

Mom and Dad you guys work so hard
to have a roof on top of my head
to have food to eat
to have a bed to sleep in
and to have everything I want

You guys are so beautiful to my eyes
you guys look like the sun
you are so precious to me
I will always love you until I die
I love you Mom and Dad.

Marven Rincon is a 7th grader and is currently attending Ann Richards Middle School. Marven Issac Rincon Vasquez in his free time he likes to write about his family.

The Faltering Leaf
Felix Solis lll

The leaf falters with the touch of cold
as the snow starts to grow,
autumns frost arrived trickling the trees in white
and made the leaves fall in fright.

But there stood a brave leaf
never faltering at all
as the cold froze the waters to white.
But the little girl watched as the leaf
never faltered at all.
She smiled and laughed as people
sang their canciones
lasting all night long.

She always looked out as if reaching a hand,
and giving warmth to the leaf
at last.

But the cold sept into her room, freezing her, too.
Yet the leaf brave as ever
Never left her alone.
As the snow grew.
She seemed to grow frail.
All because of the frosty fright.
She cried night after night.
But the leaf was always in her sight.
Until that last night.
A trickle of snow left the air and spring leapt it's,
Way into the air as the leaf stood and watched.
The girl finally stood up.
And with a warmth to her face.
She gave the leaf a hug as she waved away.

Felix Solis lll is an 8th grader and is currently attending Ann Richards Middle School. Felix Solis lll in his free time likes to draw.

BOUNDLESS
AUTHOR BIOS

Dr. Grisel Y. Acosta's (she/they) first poetry book is *Things to Pack on the Way to Everywhere*. Their work is in *Poetry Magazine, Acentos Review*, and beyond. She is the editor of *Latina Outsiders* (Routledge, 2019), Creative Writing Editor at *Chicana/Latina Studies Journal*, and a Poetry Editor at *WSQ Journal*.

Dahlia Aguilar, of Corpus Christi is an emergent writer in her fifties. An alum of Under the Volcano (2024, 2025), her poems appear in *The Skinny Poetry Journal, Acentos Review, Somos Xicanas* and *Boundless 2024*. She lives in Deanwood, Washington, D.C. with her son, two dogs and menopause.

Alejandra Sánchez Alanís, host of *Platica y Poetics* is a queer translingual/ bilinual poet, songwriter, radio DJ, and abstract artist whose work transcends the boundaries of language, music, and art. Their storytelling is deeply rooted in sensory experiences, merging the auditory, poetic, and visual into a lush tapestry of artistic expression. Drawing from their background as a language teacher and music mixer, she explores the musicality and visual elements of poetry, treating white space as a form of foreplay—an invitation to indulge in the hypnotic rhythms of sensory pleasure with a lyrical nature, seamlessly blending translanguaging and intricate sensory details to create immersive, multilingual spaces where readers and listeners can coexist. The intersection of the senses— auditory, poetic, and visual—making their work a layered experience further amplifying queer voices and artistic expression inviting readers and listeners to explore the pleasure of language and art.

Naomi Alegre is a Mexican American poet born and raised in Brownsville, Texas. Alegre works as an Editorial Associate for a multimedia platform. Alegre hopes to one day turn poetry into her full-time job.

Steve Anc is the son of Ajuzie Nwaorisa and he is a Nigerian poet. He is a Pushcart Prize Nominee. He has a searching knowledge and deep meditation on some universal themes. He is a modern poet and his adherence to language and his use of metaphor is soul-searching.

Anc is the author of Nine poetry anthologies with a tenth forthcoming anthology (Soul to Soul: Poetry of Life, Light, and Brokenness). His poetry has been featured in several recent magazines and journals, such as the American University of Iraq, Sulaimani among others.

Sandra Arenas has a bachelor's degree in English Literature by UNAM and is a member of the research collective Poetica Sonora MX since 2022. Currently, she is a scholarship recipient of the songwriting workshop at SACM. Her texts have been published at different print and online publications.

This work submitted by author Mr. **Fernando Baeza** was a last minute entry. The author debated whether or not to enter such an intimate piece as the origin is no mystery. The letter holds no edits or liberties and was handed as is. The young lady held no objections and conceded to publish *Tu Marea*. Mr. Fernando Baeza is a man of letters and holds a degree in English Literature. His hobbies include painting and among his daily readings include poetry giants Rimbaud, Baudelaire and Dante.

Hongwei Bao (he/him) is a queer Chinese writer and academic based in Nottingham, UK. He is the author of the poetry pamphlet *Dream of the Orchid Pavilion* (Big White Shed Press 2024) and the poetry collection *The Passion of the Rabbit* God (Valley Press, 2024).

Analyssa Beltran is an English teacher based in South Texas, where she inspires her students with a passion for literature and storytelling. She earned her degree in Literature from SUNY Albany and holds an M.A.T. from Bard College. Analyssa's writing delves into the complexities of Latina identity, often exploring the unique struggles of those who feel marginalized within their own culture. Through her short stories, she brings to life the nuanced and deeply personal experiences of women navigating the intersection of heritage, expectation, and self-discovery.

Victor Benavides,an English teacher and writer from the south Texas borderlands. Benavidez teaches High School English and College Prep in Brownsville, Texas

Xochitl-Julisa Bermejo is the daughter of Mexican immigrants and author of *Incantation: Love Poems for Battle Sites* (Mouthfeel Press) and *Posada: Offerings of Witness and Refuge* (Sundress Publications). A former Steinbeck Fellow and *Poets & Writers* California Writers Exchange winner, she's received residencies from Hedgebrook, Ragdale, Jentel, Yefe Nof, and National Parks Arts Foundation in partnership with Gettysburg National Military Park and Poetry Foundation. Her poem "Battlegrounds" was featured at Academy of American Poets' *Poem-a-Day,* On Being's *Poetry Unbound,* and the anthology, *Poetry Unbound: 50 Poems to Open Your World* (W.W. Norton). Her poetry can be found at *Acentos Review,*

Huizache, Santa Fe Writers Project, and other journals. She teaches poetry and creative writing with Antioch University, MFA and UCLA Extension and is the director of Women Who Submit.

Kemberly Borrego is a writer and student whose poetry explores themes of love, loss, and the human experience. With a passion for emotional depth and introspection, she crafts words that resonate with vulnerability and connection. Through her work, Kemberly seeks to evoke empathy and spark meaningful reflection in her readers.

Julie Brandon is a poet, playwright and short story writer, Her work has appeared in numerous publications including Bewildering Stories, Detangled Brains, Altered Reality, Witcraft, Bright Flash Fiction, Flash Phantoms among others. Julie's book of poetry, *My Tears, Like Rain*, was published June 2024. She lives in Illinois.

Katrenia Grace Busch is an award-winning poet, freelance journalist and author whose works have appeared in CBS, NPR, Red Penguin Books, Bloom Magazine, Flash Fiction Friday among others and continues to serve as a poetry editor for The Bookends Review, editor for the American Psychological Association and federal grant reviewer.

Reyes Cárdenas was born and raised in Seguin, Texas. His books of poetry include Survivors of the Chicano Titanic, I Was Never A Militant Chicano, Chicano Poet- Poems 1970-2010, Tortured Barrio Songs, and the forthcoming collection Flirting With The Past. Blog: chicanopoet.blogspot.com

Aldo Cristian Méndez Castillo nació en Ciudad Valles, San Luis Potosí, México, el 06 de octubre de 1980. Su pasión principal es escribir poesía en español y en inglés. Algunos textos de su autoría han sido publicados en antologías como "Boundless 2023", "Amor y Desamor 2023", "Locos contadores de historias", "Antología de terror volumen 4", "Puedo, soy, existo", "Memorias del olvido", "Boundless 2024", "Poetas mexicanos" entre otras.

Iván Medina Castro nació en México. Tiene cinco libros publicados: *En cualquier lugar fuera de este mundo, Más frío que la muerte, Lugares ajenos, Caminos irreverentes,* y *La hija del gallero.* Becario del FONCA-CONACYT (2012) y (2024). Será parte de la residencia artística *Under the Volcano* 2025 https://underthevolcano.org/

Adrian Ernesto Cepeda is the author of 6 poetry collections. *La Lengua Inside Me* with FlowerSong Press won Honorable Mention in The Juan Felipe Herrera Best Book Award in The 2024 Int'l Latino Book Awards.

Adrian lives with his wife in Los Angeles and their adorably spoiled cat Woody Gold.

Mayurakshi Chaturvedi is a poet from Kolkata, India. She has performed at open mics all over the world like the New York Public Library, the University of Cambridge, Sarah Lawrence College, etc. Her poems have appeared in various anthologies, published by Georgetown University, Bishop's University, Beyond the Veil Press, etc.

Rogelio de Jesús Cisneros. Psicólogo y psicoanalista, tiene una especialidad en Literatura y Creación Literaria por el Universitario Bauhaus. Ha participado como comentarista en ciclos de cine, como ensayista y poeta en revistas literarias y antologías. Participó en la antología poética "Habitantes" (Feria internacional del libro Coahuila, México 2023). En 2024 presentó su primer poemario "Las horas del aire" (Conversing through poetry, Houston, Texas).

Arturo Cortez Jr. was born and resides in the RGV. He lived in Rio Bravo, Tamaulipas until the age of 14. He engages mainly in topics of coming of age, identity and hometown nostalgia. His poetry has been published in the anthology *Boundless 2024* and *Solstice Literary Magazine* (Winter 2024).

PW Covington is the NBPF's 'New Mexico Beat Poet Laureate' (2024-2026). Covington has spent decades traveling the highways of North America sharing his work and encouraging the work of others.

A former VIPF Featured Poet, in 2019, his collection *North Beach and Other Stories* was named a Finalist in LGBTQ Fiction from the International Book Awards. Covington lives just south of Historic Route 66 in Albuquerque, New Mexico, where he has worked on film and television projects including *Better Call Saul* and *Ransom Canyon*.

Heather Cathleen Cox is an investigative journalist and photojournalist with bylines appearing in *Yahoo! News, NewsBreak, The Times of Israel* and *Jerusalem Post*. In 2023, her creative nonfiction story, "Becoming Esther," was anthologized.

A poetess and singer-songwriter, she leads both poetry workshops and open mic events in Texas and abroad.

Linda M. Crate (she/her) is a Pennsylvanian writer whose poetry, short stories, articles, and reviews have been published in a myriad of magazines both online and in print. She has twelve published chapbooks the latest being: *Searching Stained Glass Windows For An Answer* (Alien Buddha Publishing, December 2022).

Doug Croft has multiple anthology and journal credits. His first full-length poetry collection, *Exposed Roots*, was published in 2023. Croft resides in Charlotte, from where he travels to work projects as a professional fundraising campaign counsel, and to see as many of his favorite rock 'n' roll bands as possible.

Christopher T. Dabrowski is a Polish writer and screenwriter. His books have been published in Poland, the USA, Canada, Spain, Germany and India. www.krzysztoftdabrowsk.wixsite.com/krzysztoftdabrowski

Charles Darnell lives in San Antonio, TX. He is a member of the Maverick Poetry Group. His poems have appeared in many journals, anthologies, and magazines most recently in Central Texas Writer's Anthology, Voices De La Luna, and The Waco Wordfest anthology. His chapbook, *Water, Tongues, Earth, and Blood* was published in 2018. His full volume of poetry, *Toward Human*, in 2022.

Kim Denning is a Latina poet from Texas who practices curanderismo in the footsteps of her ancestral abuelas and likes to play the guitar very loudly. Her poetry has been published in various online and print publications.

William Derge's poems have appeared in Negative Capability, The Bridge, Artful Dodge, Bellingham Review, and other publications. He is the winner of the 2010 Knightsbridge Prize and winner of the Rainmaker Award. He received honorable mentions in contests sponsored by The Bridge, Sow's Ear, and New Millennium.

Logan Dovalina is an emerging author from the Rio Grande Valley. His upcoming publication, *Una Vida Moderna: Self Discovery and Architecture in the Texas-Mexico Borderlands*, will be published in 2025. He holds bachelor's and master's degrees in Integrative Studies from the University of North Texas.

DUGGAN is an Irish writer and poet who happens to be autistic. DUGGAN chooses to identify as an autistic poet because so many misconceptions exist about those with autism, and so few autistic voices are represented in the arts.

DUGGAN's poems have been published in a variety of journals including Rattle Magazine, Savoy Magazine and Planet Ireland; and in anthologies including 'Colours of the Moon' (Mosaique Press), 'Fate' (HH Press), 'Poems of Hope' (Samaritans Press), and 'Chance' (AUB Press). In the past 12 months poems by DUGGAN were shortlisted for the Artemesia Poetry Prize, the Arts University Bournemouth International Poetry Prize, and the Hammond House International Literary Prize.

Guy S Duke is a nonbinary poet, photographer, artist, and archaeologist originally from Western Canada, now living in McAllen, TX. They have been writing for over three decades, self-publishing the zines Collective Insanity in Canada the '90s and early '00s and Gender Non-Compliant in Texas in summer 2024.

Emmanuel Con Dos Emmes, an illustrator and poet from Veracruz, Mexico, has lived in McAllen, Texas, for 13 years. Passionate about Spanish-speaking poetry, his work is inspired by Latin American magical realism and children's songs and stories. He serves on the board of Unfolded: Poetry Project, established in McAllen.

Alejandro Zapata Espinosa (Itagüí, Colombia, 2002): licenciado en Literatura y Lengua Castellana del Tecnológico de Antioquia.

Anne Estevis was raised in Corpus Christi, but spent many years in New Mexico where she met her South Texas husband. They eventually returned to Texas. Estevis has published fiction, poetry, essays, and memoirs. She is retired from the University of Texas system.

Ziying Fan, a software engineer and 2019 Princeton graduate, is currently pursuing a Masters in Comparative Literature at Oxford University. Xuelan and Ziying's translations have appeared in LIT magazine, NW Linguist and Book of Matches.

Abdulrozaq Tasleem Fholarin, is a poet who hails from the south-western part of Nigeria, and writes the thin line between the paradox of life, death. He writes about nature too. His works have been published in The Kalahari review and Jay lit magazine. When he is not writing, he reads poems, or academic books, or recedes to his part-time teaching job, or engages in something lively.

Jonathan Fletcher holds a Master of Fine Arts in Creative Writing from Columbia University. A Pushcart Prize, Best of the Net, and Best Microfiction nominee, he won Northwestern University Press's Drinking Gourd Chapbook Poetry Prize contest in 2023. *This is My Body*, his debut chapbook, will be published in 2025.

Immanuel A. Garcia is a Queer & Hispanic writer from Denton, TX. He is the author of 2 collections of poetry: *Pèace De Résistance ['17]*, and *Under Wannabe Moonlight ['24]*. A multi-time slam poetry champion, he was also named the 2024 Story Slam Champion per the 39th Annual Texas Storytelling Festival.

Belén Thérèse Garza Flores is a writer and editor in the Río Grande Valley. She graduated with an MFA in Creative Writing from UTRGV. She writes essays on her WordPress blog, Ojalá Ojalá:Essays from the Valley of Tears. These essays examine Mexican American culture from a Valley Catholic perspective.

Kevin Adam Flores is a Hispanic American poet and short-story writer. He has been published in The Twin Bill, The Hole in the Head Review, Too Well Away, Superpresent, and Fleas on the Dog. He recently released his first book titled *Bittersweet and Blue*. The author resides in South Texas.

Suranjit Gain, Born on 8 October in 1984 Khulna district in Bangladesh. Mother Lila Gain. Father Tapan Gain. Primary education from Dacope saheberabad primary school. Secondary from Herovanga Vidyasagar Vidyamandir, West Bengal, India. Higher secondary from Gobordanga Collegiate High School, India.

The creation of literature begins from childhood. Priest (gurudev) world famous poet Purushottam Kazi Nazrul Islam. Number of published books is about one hundred and fifty. Bengali, Hindi, English, Sanskrit literature published from several countries of the world. maximum writings and books released with the finance of publication. Admired and recognized by international literary festivals. National and international awarded poet. Congratulations from the universe in literature.

Clara Elena García is a Paraguayan-born poet based in Upstate New York. Her first book, "Juego de Palabras," was published in May 2023 with Valparaiso Ediciones. Her second book, "Seven Legendary Monsters" is forthcoming in Spring 2025 from Revolutionaries Press.

Lisha Adela García resides in San Antonio, Texas with her four-legged children. She is the Author of *This Stone Will Speak*, *Blood Rivers* and *A Rope of Luna*. She is widely published. Lisha is a Certified Poetic Medicine Practitioner and the Poetry Editor for *Voices de La Luna* literary journal.

Ruth Garcia is a 21 year old college graduate still figuring out life. She loves to paint and take long walks with her dog, sometimes cooking if there's no other option. More than anything, she loves sitting and watching the sunset.

Lilia K. Garza is a recent graduate student of Memorial High School who has been writing poetry for 2 years. Her interests are astronomy, physics, reading novels, drawing, US history and its politics, and environmental preservation.

Violeta Garza is a Latinx poet, artist, and performer from San Antonio, TX. Her debut poetry chapbook *Brava* was a semifinalist for the 2023 Nine Syllables Press Chapbook Contest, and will be released in September 2025 by First Matter Press. You can peruse their work at violetagarza.com.

Michael Gerleman is a retired English teacher who has lived in the Rio Grande valley for 37 years.

Edward K Gonzales, born in Northeast Los Angeles, currently living in El Paso TX. Living my life with what my mother called the Texas way. She was a no-nonsense straight shooter, as am I. I have been writing my whole life in the form of Journaling and prose. Recently a member of the Sun Poet Society And currently a member of The Maverick Poetry Group and El Paso Workshop group.

Joann González descends from a strong line of women. Her voice, more than just her own, represents the voices of her foremothers. Joann writes so that voice remains alive, not only in her but inside other strong women alike.

John Grey is an Australian poet, US resident, recently published in New World Writing, New English Review and Tenth Muse. Latest books, "Subject Matters", "Between Two Fires" and "Covert" are available through Amazon. Work upcoming in Haight-Ashbury Literary Journal, Amazing Stories and River and South.

Carlo R. Guinita is a license Agricultural Engineer by profession. He resides at

Brgy. San Roque, Digos City, Davao del Sur, Philippines. He took on jobs as college instructor and a senior high school teacher. His first poetry pieces were accepted at Poet But Us. He writes as his hobby and passion.

Barbara Gurney is based in a suburb of Perth, Western Australia. She writes across several genres including free verse poetry and fiction prose for adults and children. Barbara's poetry delves into emotions both solemn and hopeful with conviction, while often exploring a fragile connection to the environment. www.barbaragurney.com

Nianna E. Gustovich is a linguist versed in English, French, and Spanish and uses the vibrancy of her language experience to enrich her poetry and teaching. She believes that one should always continue adding verses to your life.

Danielle Harvey is from San Diego, California and now lives in Austin, Texas. Danielle writes poetry in her free time focussing on bringing to light individual and the collective challenges of the world including mental health, religion, and grief. Her goal is to continue to use poetry as an outlet for personal and collective healing and growth.

Hayden is a Mom, Humanities Professor, Animal Rescuer, and Poet Laureate. Her debut collection, American Saunter, released December 2025 by FlowerSong Press. Her first chapbook, *How to Tie Tobacco*, as well as her second full-length collection, *Old World Wings*, will be released in 2025. She lives with her family and rescues, including a very special blind, three-legged pup named Vinny Valentine.

Cynthia Hernandez is a Chicana, mother, and poet. Hernandez won the 2023 Journal X Best Poetry Award with *Hungry to Learn*. She is also published in The LA Poet Society's *Acid Verse II, The Earth Beneath Our Feet*, as well as in Southwestern College's The Other Writers Guild, *The Vagabond*.

Joel Hinojosa, McAllen, TX, has been inspired by the art of language since very young. Words are his muse, and he enjoys creating honest, impactful work. His work explores themes of identity, self-discovery, and culture.

A Hua, born Wang Xiaohua, is from Weihai, Shandong province, China. She is a much-loved, award-winning poet in China. Her poetry is published in numerous journals and several anthologies. Her two collections, "Cattails" (2016) and "What Makes My Heart Swell" (2021), are published by Shandong Art & Literature Publishing House, Ltd.

Gabriela Iñiguez, obtained an MFA in Creative Writing from San José State University. Her poems have appeared in *Tiferet Journal*, *Moonstone Press*, and más allá de las palabras. Her flash fiction was selected to participate in the IV Anthology of the FIL de la Ciudad de Nueva York.

"**Feroza Jussawalla** is a retired Professor of English, from India, who has made the U.S. Southwestern region her home for the last forty years. Her name literally means "Turquoise Silversmith." She believes there is something serendipitous in her ending up in the South West. She considers herself, both Indian and Chicana. She has a Ph.D from the University of Utah, where she came as an exchange student. She has taught at the University of Texas at El Paso, and at the University of New Mexico. She is the author, or, co- editor of several scholarly books and articles".

Sidney King is a freshman biology student at the University of Texas Rio Grande Valley and has long fostered a love for the written word. Sidney is working towards one day becoming an ornithologist and plans on studying seabirds.

Edward Lee's poetry, short stories, non-fiction and photography have been published in magazines in Ireland, England and America, including The Stinging Fly, Skylight 47, Acumen, The Blue Nib and Poetry Wales. His poetry collections include *A Foetal Heart, Bones Speaking With Hard Tongues, To Touch The Sky And Never Know The Ground Again* and *The Heart As Dust Lost In The Wind.*

He also makes musical noise under the names Ayahuasca Collective, Orson Carroll, Lego Figures Fighting, and Pale Blond Boy. His blog/website can be found at https://edwardmlee.wordpress.com

Alexander Limarev, freelance artist, mail art artist, poet, visual poet and curator from Russia/Siberia. Participated in more than 1000 international projects and exhibitions. His artworks are part of private and museum collections of 74 countries. His artworks as well as poetry have been featured in various online publications including BUKOWSKI ERASURE POETRY ANTHOLOGY (Silver Birch Press), MAINTENANT, NEW FEATHERS ANTHOLOGY, EKPHRASTIC REVIEW etc.

Felicia Lopez is an award winning RGV author with her debut self-published book called "In Space and Time" available on Amazon. She is passionate about reading, writing, and storytelling. She strives to inspire others through captivating narratives and life experiences.

Max Tyrone Lozano is a writer from the Rio Grande Valley. His poetry has been featured in Rigorous, samfiftyfour, as well as Gallery. His work focuses on the intersections of race, class, and border identities.

Bill Mainous has poems appearing in Odes and Elegies, The Windward, Clinch Mountain Review and several others. He works in healthcare and as a tutor. Currently working on a Masters in Creative Writing. Mainous hold degrees in both English and History. He lives in Edinburg, Texas.

Mariana Mcdonald is a poet, writer, and activist. Her poetry, fiction, and essays have appeared in numerous publications, including *Crab Orchard Review, Ceasefire Now!, Sargasso, The Poet, Antología de la Poesía Viequense, Lunch Ticket, The New Verse News, About Place Journal, Poesía en Vuelo,* and *Anthology of Southern Poets.* She co-authored *Dominga Rescues the Flag,* the story of Black Puerto Rican heroine Dominga de la Cruz. Mcdonald became a Hambidge Arts Center fellow in 2012 and was appointed a Black Earth Institute Scholar/Fellow for 2022-2025. She loves Earth, justice, Puerto Rico, *Nueva Trova,* and black cats. She lives in Atlanta.

Joselin Mejía (México, 1993). Her poems have been anthologized in Boundless 2021, 2022, 2023 and 2024: The Anthology of the Rio Grande Valley International Poetry Festival (Texas, USA, FlowerSong Press). Her poetry has also been published in Mexico, Colombia and Chile. In 2024 she participated in the Third Anniversary of the Real Academia Internacional de Arte y Literatura; also in the IV International Poetry Meeting in Xochimilco. In 2023 was part of the II Cycle of poetic readings: La piel verdadera, actual Mexican poetry written by women.

Walter Alexis Velásquez Mendoza: Seudónimo: **Arthur Haneke,** 27 años. Bachiller de la carrera de Periodismo en la Universidad Antonio Ruiz de Montoya. Trabaja en redes sociales en el Instituto ILEN y editor web en Contigo TV. Participó en el proyecto de un guión de una película peruana de comedia (al final no se dio luz verde para el avance) y fue columnista de cine en el Diario UNO. También es escritor y ganador de diversos concursos literarios. Ha sido ganador del concurso literario COVID-19: memorias de confinamiento de la Editorial Almandino en la categoría crónica, mención honrosa en el concurso de microrrelatos de la fundación literaria Letraviva (Colombia) y mención honrosa en el concurso literario del podcast El Buen Cruel (México). Recientemente ha dictado talleres de redacción periodística y microcuento (en la librería Ciudad Librera con próxima a realizar una segunda edición). Vive en Lima, Perú.

Victoria Montes was born in Seattle, Washington and moved to McAllen, Texas when she was five years old, where she currently lives. Her roommates are one dog and a bossy cat named TinkerBelle. You can find her on instagram and threads @whitelotusflower21.

Guna Moran is an internationally acclaimed Assamese poet and book reviewer. His poems are published in 300 hundred international magazines, journals, webzines, blogs, newspapers, anthologies. Some of them are Indian Literature, Indian Poetry Review, Indian Review, Indian Periodical , Muse India, Outlook, International Writer's Journal, International Times Magazine, AZAHAR Revista Poetica, The Poet Magazine, The Global Youth Review, Whatcom Watch Newspaper, Spillword, Merak Magazine, Quidditty, Lovina 103, Indiana University Press, The California Times Newspaper, Poetry Hall, The Piker Press, Bario Blues Press, North eastern University Journal, The Tiger Moth Magazine, World Contemporary Poets Vol 1. He has won Creator Of Justice Award 2020 by International Human Right Art Festival and got a chance for reading poetry in Frankfurt Book Fair 2020 (Digital edition). His poems have already been translated into Croatian, Tagalog (Philippines), Burmese, Swahili (Kenya), Indonesian, Italian, French, Spanish, Portuguese, Macedonian, Chinese, Ukrainian, Russian, Hebrew, Turkish, Hindi, Tamil, Telegu, Marathi, Urdu, Gujrati, Arabic, Bengali. He has published three poetry books to his credit. They are - When The Tree Weeps, Time Will Write History On You, El Amor - Love On The Rocks (Jointly). He is invited to join poetry programme organised by America, Hong Kong, Bangladesh, Mumbai, Delhi, Andhra Pradesh, West Bangla, Panorama International Literature Festival 2022, VI Open Eurasian Literary Festival Of Festivals " Lift " 2022 and many more.

José Luis Moreno, no es un poeta, es un aficionado a la poesía clásica de arte mayor y menor. Es de Reynosa Tamaulipas. Cuenta con un libro publicado *La Poesía pide la palabra* y escribe para la revista Ecos Literarios, José Luis Calderón Vela de León Guanajuato. En 1923 flower song press en la antología Rio Grande Valley

International Poetry Festival Boundless 2023 publicó *Una plegaria más* de su autoría. **Tom Murphy** is a road poet and the 2021-2022 Corpus Christi Poet Laureate and the *Langdon Review*'s 2022 Writer-In-Residence. This will be Murphy's eight participation at V.I.P.F.. Murphy's books: *When I Wear Bob Kaufman's Eyes* (2022), *Snake Woman Moon* (2021), *Pearl* (2020), *American History* (2017), and co-edited *Stone Renga* (2017). https://tommurphywriter.com

Adela Najarro's fifth poetry collection, *Variations in Blue*, was selected by the Letras Latinas/ Red Hen Collaborative and is currently available. The California Arts Council recognized her as an established artist for the Central California Region, appointing her as a 2023 Individual Artist Fellow. Learn more at www. adelanajarro.com

Crischelle Navalta identifies as an Ilocana-Filipina American, educator, and immigrant. She is based in Edinburg, and has been an educator in the RGV for 20 years. Crischelle loves to garden and travel with her family to connect with friends and relatives around the US and in the Philippines. Most of her writing is autobiographical, about daily life, and experiences in nature.

David Ndubuisi is an emerging poet with a unique voice that captures the depth of human emotion and cultural heritage. Originally from Nigeria, David began writing his poetry at an early age. Balancing personal insight with universal themes, his work often explores identity, resilience, and the beauty of everyday life. Driven by a desire to reach more readers, he is working on his debut poetry collection, aiming to bring his thoughts and stories to the wider world. David's poetry resonates with readers who seek authenticity and raw emotion in the written word.

Originally from Jalisco, México, **Osmani Ochoa** is a queer poet and a national organizer for immigrant & worker rights, living in San Antonio, TX. His poetry mixes themes of immigration, borders, class, race, and multilingualism. They have been accepted for publication in Space & Time Magazine, Cuéntame Literary Magazine, Windward Review, La Raíz Magazine and was a finalist for the 2024 Howling Bird Press Poetry Prize and shortlisted for the Abode Press chapbook prize.

Osmani is featured in two forthcoming Latino sci-fi anthologies: "Not Your Papi's Utopia: Latinx Visions of Radical Hope" edited by Matthew David Goodwin, Alex Hernández, and Sara Rivera (Mouthfeel Press) and "Chicanofuturism Now! Visions of a Raza Future" edited by Scott Russell Duncan (Riot of Roses Press).

Joseph C Ogbonna is a prolific poet from Nigeria. He is very widely published. He has some of his works published in magazines, anthologies, journals and in online blogs. His works had been aired by the BBC Radio 3. He lives in Enugu, Nigeria.

John Chinaka Onyeche is a Nigerian writer of colour (BIPOC) and historian from Etche in Rivers State. A graduate of history and diplomatic studies. He serves as a poetry curator with Port Harcourt Literary Review. He is dedicated to ensuring that the full scope of history is accurately represented. His writing can be found in various journals, including; Charles University, Prague, Ebedi Review, Overtly Lit, Middlebury Institute of International Studies, McNeese University, Pier Review University of Brighton, Tilted House Journal, Akewi Magazine, and Brittle Paper. Connect with him on Twitter @Apostlejohnchin or https://linker. ee/RememberAjc

TEDx Speaker **Daniel García Ordaz**, a.k.a. The Poet Mariachi, served as the 2023 McAllen Poet Laureate and will continue in this honorary post in 2024-2025. His work has been taught and written about by academics across the U.S. and abroad and he is a 2018 Pushcart Prize nominee. García earned an MFA in Creative Writing, a terminal degree, from The University of Texas Rio Grande Valley. He is also a high school English teacher and part of the dual enrollment faculty at South Texas College. García is a songwriter, and former journalist. García appears in the documentary, "ALTAR: Cruzando fronteras/Building bridges." He is the founder of the Rio Grande Valley Int'l. Poetry Festival.

Born in Galveston, **Michael Owens** is a botanist by training and writes from his home in Cypress Texas. Michael's work has been included in publications; Metonym Literary Journal at Jessup University, Red River Review, Houston Chronicle-After Harvey Poems, Poetica 2-by Clarendon, House Publications, Austin International Poetry Society, Houston Poetry Fest.

Demian Palacios (México, 1990) In 2024 he published his second book La lluvia de los quetzales by Buenos Aires Poetry. He published his first book in 2018 Donde se hiela la sal del mar (Mexico, Ediciones Del lirio). He published in the Naufrago Magazine presented at the 7th International Book Fair of Arquetipica, Peru. His poems have been antologised in Boundless 2024: The Anthology of the Rio Grande Valley International Poetry Festival, the Real Academia de Internacional de Arte y Literatura, UNAM and Verso Destierro.

Julia-Paz, Monte Alto, TX, has been writing her whole life: creative writing, research, and her favorite poetry. She has taken the time to develop what she calls "conversations" between her pen and paper. Her poetry reflects personal experiences and cultural heritage, inspiring others to express themselves creatively.

Bernard Pearson's work appears in over one hundred publications worldwide, including; *Aesthetica Magazine* , *The Edinburgh Review,*and *Crossways*. In 2017 a selection of his poetry 'In Free Fall' was published by *Leaf by Leaf Press*. In 2019 he won second prize in The Aurora Prize for Writing for his poem *Manor Farm*.

Laura Peña is an award winning poet born and raised in Houston, Tx. She holds a BA in English Literature and an MA in Education. She is a primary bilingual teacher as well as a translator of poetry into Spanish. Laura has been a featured poet at Valley International Poetry Festival, Inprint First Fridays, and Public Poetry. She has been published both in print and on-line journals. She has been a workshop presenter at VIPF in the Rio Grande Valley, Tx. and People's Literary Festival in Corpus Christi, Tx.. One of Laura's annual traditions is to write a poem a day for August Postcard Poetry Festival and has participated in the fest for the last 12 years.

Juan Manuel Pérez, a Mexican-American poet of Indigenous descent and the Poet Laureate for Corpus Christi, Texas (2019-2020), is the author of numerous poetry books. Please check out his official website at: https://www.juanmperez.com/.

RescuePoetix is a self-taught bilingual, internationally published performing poet, workshop facilitator, teaching and recording artist. She is twice honored Poet Laureate: first Puerto Rican Poet Laureate (Jersey City, NJ 2020-2022), State of NJ Beat Poet Laureate (2022-2024). She develops a body of work focused on community and social justice. https://linktr.ee/rescuepoetix

Kathy Trenfield Raines, a happily retired English teacher, has published poems and essays in *Boundless, Interstice, Escuchame, Voices From the Chicho* and *Along the River 2*, and *Odes and Elegies*. She has also published a Master's Thesis on Mark Twain's "The Mysterious Stranger" manuscripts. Currently, she writes a monthly column, *Creatures Among Us,* for Port Isabel/South Padre Press's *Parade* insert, each featuring a different creature from the Rio Grande Valley.

Connie Ramírez is a writer and visual artist from East Chicago, IN. She has written several essays, poems, and short stories in both English and Spanish. Previous works have been published by The Acentos Review & LabelMeLatino. com. You can find her artwork on redbubble.com under "Conboncita".

Ron Ramírez has dedicated over thirty years to Bilingual Education and worked on meeting the needs of diverse students across the Rio Grande Valley in Texas. He was a teacher and a librarian. He is a children's book author, a cultural novella writer, and a literacy concierge. He believes in literacy for all.

Myra Tejada Rasmussen is an Adjunct Professor in Creative Writing at UNCW. She received her BA in English from Notre Dame and her MFA in poetry from UNCW. A semi-finalist for the James Applewhite Poetry Prize and finalist for the Poet's Billow Pangaea Poetry Prize, she is published in Home Planet News Issue 11.

Ramiro Hernández Restrepo (Medellín, Colombia, 1958): , hijo de Raquel y Emilio, profesional en derecho y ciencias políticas. Participó del XXI Encuentro de Poetas de Comfenalco Antioquia (2022) y de la separata nro. 6 de la *Revista Literaria Trinando* (Colombia-México, 2023).

Eduardo Villarreal De Los Reyes. Seudónimo: Chaneque. En 1985, candidato del CREA por el estado de Nuevo León al Premio Nacional de la Juventud. Aparece en los libros "Poetas de Ayer y Hoy en Tamaulipas" (1985), compilado por Ramón Durón Ruiz e "Historia de la Literatura en Tamaulipas (1985), editado por la Universidad Autónoma de Tamaulipas. En 1996, El Festival de Otoño (Matamoros, Tamaulipas) le otorga el reconocimiento "A las expresiones del arte". 2022, la Escuela Secundaria Técnica núm. 4, de la ciudad de H. Matamoros, Tamaulipas, se develó la placa del nombre de la biblioteca escolar como "Lic. Eduardo Villarreal De Los Reyes". En 2023, finalista del Premio Nacional de Poesía "Alicia Acosta". En el 2024, recibe reconocimiento en el 27 Encuentro Internacional de Poesía del Estado de México.

Libros publicados: Ahora pregunto yo (2019). || A veces la poesía (2020.). ||Todo de nuevo.(2020). Poemas cortos amores largos (2021). Viernes de Dolores (2023) y El Imperio del Olvido (2024). Colaborador en medios nacionales. Instagram: @ villarreal_delos_reyes_eduardo

Anthony Ripp considers himself a storyteller who writes his best material on the open road or sitting in the middle of an ocean in a remote part of the world. He takes his inspiration from real life events and enjoys featuring the beauty that is attached to the rusty side of life. Anthony states that he does not write to make a point, he writes to make the listeners feel something.

Líza Rivera is an entrepreneur & intuitive healer in the RGV. She recognizes the Oneness & divinity in all living beings, from the two-legged to the eight-legged. Her poetry reflects both the world she sees, and the one longs to see.

Born in "Brick City" Newark, NJ **Yari "Porta Rock"** is an educator, writer, poet and activist using his craft to transmit lessons and messages of identity and social protest to the masses. He has a book titled, "From In Between the Bricks I Rise: Reflections from a Porta Rock."

R. Joseph Rodríguez is the author of *This Is Our Summons Now: Poems* (FlowerSong Press, 2022), and his most recent book is titled *Youth Scribes: Teaching a Love of Writing* (Heinemann, 2025). He and his students are readers of borderlands literature as well as banned and challenged books. Contact: @escribescribe or escribescribe@gmail.com.

Linda Feliciana Romero is from Harlingen, Texas and has been published in *Boundless*, the anthology for the Rio Grande Valley International Poetry Festival, *Along the River 2: More Voices from the Rio Grande* (VAO Publishing), *Twenty: In Memoriam* (El Zarape Press), and *La Bloga*. She was nominated for a Pushcart Prize in 2018 for her poem, "In the Passenger Seat" by El Zarape Press which appeared in *Boundless* 2017. Linda has a private practice as a dyslexia therapist, and is a board member of the International Dyslexia Association - Austin branch.

Jio De La Rosa is a mother, writer, and educator in the Rio Grande Valley. Her love of pop-culture, sci-fi, fantasy, and gothic literature paints the edges of her writing, always. Lately, she has been using her rage as a form of resistance. And, she likes it. She likes it a lot.

Rosalva Ruiz was born in Weslaco, Texas in 1981. She started writing as a way to express herself. Member of "Codice Colectivo Literario and some of her works have been published in national and international anthologies as well as international ezines.

Miriam Sagan is the author of over thirty books of poetry, fiction, and memoir. She is a two-time winner of the New Mexico/Arizona Book Awards as well as a recipient of the City of Santa Fe Mayor's Award for Excellence in the Arts and a New Mexico Literary Arts Gratitude Award. She has been a writer in residence in four national parks, Yaddo, MacDowell, Gullkistan in Iceland, Kura Studio in Japan, and a dozen more remote and interesting places. She works with text and sculptural installation as part of the mother/daughter creative team Maternal Mitochondria (with Isabel Winson-Sagan) in venues ranging from RV parks to galleries. She founded and directed the creative writing program at Santa Fe Community College until her retirement. Her poetry was set to music for the Santa Fe Women's Chorus, incised on stoneware for two haiku pathways, and projected as video inside an abandoned building during the pandemic under the auspices of Vital Spaces.

Edgar Salazar nací en Monterrey Nuevo León, pero vivo en Los Fresnos, TX . Empecé a escribir a los 14 años, principalmente para expresar mis pensamientos y emociones. No comparte mucho de mi trabajo, pero la escritura me ayuda conectarme con sí mismo y reflexionar sobre mis experiencias.

Ben Salinas is a writer and educator based in Edinburg, Texas. His writing is concerned with the concept of "ownership" of identity, land and art.

Danilah De Los Santos currently in 9th grade, at Medical Professions Olmito Texas enjoys poetry, art and currently studying to become a pharmacist. She also loves cats and baking for loved ones

Carl Scharwath, has appeared globally with 180+ journals selecting his writing or art. Carl has published four poetry books and his latest book is "The World Went Dark," published by Alien Buddha Press. Carl has four photography books, published with Praxis and CreatiVingenuitiy. His photography was exhibited in the Mount Dora and Leesburg Centers for the Arts. Carl is currently an art editor at Glitterati and former editor for Minute Magazine. He was nominated with four The Best of the Net Awards (2021-25) and two different 2023 Pushcart Nominations for poetry and a short story.

Rolando Serna is an award-winning Poet from La Villa Texas who loves his friends and family.

Michael Shoemaker is a poet, writer, photographer, and editor from Magna, Utah. He is the author of two poetry/photography collections, *Rocky Mountain Reflections* and *Grasshoppers in the Field*. Michael is a three-time nominee to the 2025 Best of the Net Anthology awards. He enjoys hiking and pickleball.

Braxsen Sindelar is a writer and editor with an Associate's Degree in English from Front Range Community College. He has worked and edited for the Lighthouse Writers Workshop, *Plains Paradox*, and *Howl* magazine. He has been published in *Poetry for Mental Health* and *Locust Shell Journal* for his poetry.

Megha Sood is an Award-winning Poet, Editor, Author, and Literary Activist. Literary Partner with "Life in Quarantine", Stanford University. Her writing is informed by social issues and her experience as first generation immigrant. Her poetry will be sent to the moon in collaboration with NASA/SpaceX. Link: https://linktr.ee/meghasood

Xuelan Su is a Chinese literary translator and poetry-lover living in Seattle.

Rev. Tiffany "Queen T" is a singer and poet. Her passion for the arts, the LGBTQ+ community, and ministry pushed her to start Queen T Artistry, Inc. with her wife Jen Lozano. Tiffany currently serves as a Pastor and Worship Leader at Mount Calvary Christian Church in La Feria, TX.

Érika Garza Tamez is a teacher, poet and actress from La Joya, Texas. She has a Master of Arts in Spanish from UTPA. Garza is the author of *Con alas de mariposa* and editor of *Boundless 2024*. Her writings have been published in Antología Feipol 2018, Boundless 2019-2024, among others.

Tezozomoc is a Los Angeles Chicano Essayist, Poet and 2009 Oscar Nominated Activist, internationally published and has been published by Amoxcalco Books for "I am not your Chihuahua", and by Floricanto Press, "Gashes!: Poems and Pain from the halls of injustice", a collection of poetry, ISBN-13: 978-1951088040, 9/2019. Featured nationally and internationally across zoom open virtual mics. Published in the following journals/anthologies: 2021 Boundless Anthology, 1/20/2022, MacroMicroCosm, Healing Hands, Vol 7 Issue #3, BC, Canada, 4/15/2021, Rigorous Journal, 9/21/2020, Red Earth Productions & Cultural

Work, 12/17/2019, Underwood Press, 9/9/2019, Mom Egg Review, Los Angeles Poets for Justice, 03/15/2021.

Luis Trevino was born and raised in Edinburg, part of the Rio Grande Valley. Today he's going to school at The University of Rio Grande Valley for teaching. Today writing has taken a big part of his life, and it's time for his work to be shown to the world.

Rio Grande Valley native, **Ceci M. Valdez** is an artist, educator and writer. An educator for twenty-five years she was voted 2017 High School Teacher of the Year. Mrs. Valdez's artwork has been displayed at the Texas State Capitol and she's a contributing writer/illustrator for Bold Wolf Comics.

Vito del Valle is a Chicano writer/musician from Donna, Texas located in the Rio Grande Valley. Vito's work has appeared in Boundless Anthology 2022/2023/2024, The 2023 Northwind Treasury, South Texas College - Writer's Block, and Interstice.

J. Villanueva is a Chicano poet from south Texas. Currently, J. has words featured or forthcoming in The Iowa Review, Huizache, Taco Bell Quarterly, The Acentos Review, and more. His debut chapbook, *Roadside Fruteria*, was published in June 2022 (Bullshit Lit). He earned his MFA in 2024 at the University of Texas-Rio Grande Valley.

Javier Villarreal. Profesor emérito de español. Poeta, ensayista, traductor, fotógrafo. Autor de Entre lluvia, canto y flor (2008). Su obra ha sido incluida en diferentes antologías, revistas académicas y de creación literaria. En 2016 editó el poemario Voz de amor de Servando Cárdenas. Perfiles del silencio, su más reciente poemario, apareció en 2020. Tentempiés, su obra por venir, es una colección de epigramas, poemínimos y haikús. Por ocho años fue miembro de la mesa directiva que organizaba el People's Poetry Festival en la ciudad de Corpus Christi, Texas. En la actualidad, se dedica a organizar diversos eventos literarios y a la fotografía en el sur de Texas.

Jennifer Villegas is a Houston, Texas native with a passion for history, art, and storytelling. After spending her teenage years in South Texas, she graduated from La Joya High School in 2007 and later earned a Bachelor's degree in History with a minor in American Studies from Sam Houston State University.

In 2023, Jennifer founded My Head Inkwell Press, a creative outlet for her poetry and digital art. Through her work, she explores themes of resilience and healing, drawing from her own experiences with trauma. With a focus on the complexities of women's pain, her creations aim to transform sorrow into something profoundly beautiful, illustrating the strength of the human spirit.

When she's not writing or creating, Jennifer enjoys reflecting on her journey and finding new ways to connect with others through her art.

Trevor Wainwright, a regular since 2012 less Covid, at the RGVIPF as an International Guest Poet, Trev from England writes on a variety of subjects, a regular on his own local open mic scene and takes part in historical poetry events capturing the past., submitting two poems about his early work years.

Trier Ward is a mother, poet, and scientist. She lives in Albuquerque, New Mexico. She enjoys rehabilitating wildlife and social activism. Her latest collection of poetry is The Art of Escape, which features themes of escape from prisons in our minds and spirits. It is available on Amazon or www.trierward.com.

Jeff Woodruff is a silversmith, poet, and mobile sculptor from Austin, Texas. He is a graduate of the University of Texas with a degree in English. A studio artist, his refractive crystal mobiles and jewelry have been sold at art fairs and street festivals throughout the United States.

Diosa Xochiquetzalcóatl is a spoken word poetiza and seasoned language arts educator with a B.A. in English and M.Ed. in Cross-Cultural Teaching who has been published on both sides of the US-Mexico border. Diosa X is the author of six poetry collections, with more still to come. Learn more about her at www.diosax.net.

Su Yun , Whose real name is Chen Ruizhe, he is a 16-year-old poet. He is the member of the Chinese Poetry Society. His works have been published in more than ten countries, including the poetry collections "Spreading All Things" and "Wise Language Philosophy" in China, and the poetry collection "WITH ECSTASY OF MUSING IN TRANQUILITY" in India. He won the 2024 Guido Gozzano Apple Orchard Award in Italy.

Jeannette Zallar was born on August 20th, 1987 in San Benito, Texas. Raised by Roy and Nelda Zallar, Jeannette went through hardships throughout their life. Their specialties lie within storytelling, with a focus on life and culture. Astraia Rodriguez is a pen name which honors both past and present lives.

For details, visit our website at
valleypoetryfest.org

www.ingramcontent.com/pod-product-compliance
Lightning Source LLC
Chambersburg PA
CBHW030409130626
46549CB00004B/1691